The Herbal Palate Cookbook

MAGGIE OSTER AND SAL GILBERTIE

Photographs by Maggie Oster

STOREY

A Storey Publishing Book

Storey Communications, Inc.

*The mission of Storey Communications is to serve
our customers by publishing practical information that encourages
personal independence in harmony with the environment.*

Edited by Deborah Balmuth
Cover design by Chris Hammill Paul
Interior design and production by Laurie Musick Wright
Design and production assistance by Meredith Maker
Line drawings by Brigita Fuhrmann
Drawings on page 52 by Charles Joslin
Indexed by Northwind Editorial Services
Photo on cover: Fettucine with Mushrooms, Arugla, Parsley, and Thyme (page 48).

Copyright © 1996 by Sal Gilbertie
Photographs © Maggie Oster

The information in this book is true and complete to the best of our knowledge. All
recommendations are made without guarantee on the part of the author or Storey
Communications, Inc. The author and publisher disclaim any liability in connection with the
use of this information. For additional information please contact Storey Communications, Inc.,
Schoolhouse Road, Pownal, Vermont 05261.

Storey Publishing books are available for special premium and promotional uses and for
customized editions. For further information, please call the Custom Publishing Department at
1-800-793-9396.

Printed in Canada by Transcontinental Printing
10 9 8 7 6 5 4 3 2

Library of Congress Cataloging-in-Publication Data
Oster, Maggie.
    The herbal palate cookbook / Maggie Oster and Sal Gilbertie;
photographs by Maggie Oster.
        p.   cm.
    "A Storey Publishing Book"
    Includes bibliographical references (p.) and index.
    ISBN 0-88266-915-X (hardcover : alk. paper) — ISBN 1-58017-025-0
      (pbk. : alk. paper)
        1. Cookery (Herbs)   2. Herbs.   3. Herb gardening.
        I. Gilbertie, Sal.   II. Title.
    TX819.H408797 1996
    641.6'57—dc20
                                                                    96-3203
                                                                      CIP

Contents

*For Kurt, a most patient and generous friend
and a prince among men.*
For Sybil, with her enthusiasm, belief, and friendship.
*For Nana Gilbertie—who keeps the gardens looking so great—
and for the Gardens, because they reciprocate.*

Acknowledgments

❖

We may garden for the peace and satisfaction it brings to our lives, but as solitary as the experience may be, it is also one of sharing. And no other aspect of gardening brings people together as herbs do — sharing plants and ideas of ways to use them. I am indebted to many "herb people" from whom I have learned so much and who have been so kind to me, including the members of The Herb Society of America — Kentuckiana Unit; Paulette Kruer, Peggy Leake, Steve Thieneman, Joyce Weber, and Jeanne and Donald Fisher have been especially important on this project.

As always, I am most grateful for the support of my mother, Lucille Oster, and for Ilze Meijers. I am also honored to have cooking and styling assistance from Bruce Stitt and Kurt Hampe. And the perspective laughter, and assistance of Carrye Thompson has been of immeasurable worth.— *M.O.*

A special thanks to my many herb friends and customers who have made my life with herbs so wonderfully satisfying. Thanks to those who so generously offered their property for many of our photo sessions — Coleen O'Shea and David Anderson, Mark and Gia Watkins, and Bob and Alice Marzik.

Thanks to everyone at Gilbertie's — both in Easton and in Westport, who put up with their boss and always make the extra effort to keep up with his rapid-fire pace. Thanks to Maggie for her multitalented professionalism and her persistance, deter- mination, and hard work over many, many months to complete this wonderful book.

Thanks to my family, who are always there for me with encouragement and support. And, thank you Lord, for continuing to make my life so full.— *S.G.*

We owe no small debt to our agent, Angela Miller, and to everyone at Storey Communications, especially Deborah Balmuth and Gwen Steege.

Introduction

Quite simply, fresh herbs are best. Yes, dried, frozen, or otherwise preserved herbs are better than none at all; but once you become attuned to the flavor of fresh-from-the-garden herbs, nothing else seems quite the same. Maybe you've rarely used fresh herbs, or maybe you have but want to try new ideas. Either way, the goal of this book is to offer you recipes and ideas for cultivating a palate for fresh herbs — some in very traditional recipes, and others that we hope are ways you never thought of before.

We were inspired to collaborate on this book by our desire to share the satisfaction of having fresh herbs available at your fingertips to use in healthful, exciting ways. Although our careers have taken very different paths, both of us grew up on farms in families that celebrated fresh food. Sal Gilbertie's life as both a wholesale grower and a retail garden center operator has given him firsthand knowledge of hundreds of different herbs, as well as experience in what makes herbs grow well. A gentleman and a farmer, Sal is no gentleman farmer. Rising at the crack of dawn, he focuses his attention on every detail of the business, which has made him one of the premier wholesale suppliers of herbs. His is a family operation; his octogenarian mother still helps out in the store, and his children are involved in the business. His wife, Marie, keeps everybody on track in innumerable ways.

But put Sal in a kitchen, and you'll see that his skill with herbs doesn't stop in the field or greenhouse. An Italian heritage means that wonderfully redolent pastas take center stage, and dinner table conversation often centers around favorite dishes made by relatives and "Have you ever tried X with Y?"

Sal tells about how in his early days herbs were mainly produced for sale in the spring months. Then, in the mid-1980s people really began to get the fresh-herb habit. He saw the disappointment of people trying to grow herbs from little gift packs of tiny pots and hard-to-start seeds. They came to Gilbertie's retail shop wanting to know what went wrong. As he counseled how to successfully grow herbs in containers, he began to stock more and more pots and wooden containers as well as the best kind of potting soil mix to meet the demand. His innovative pre-planted containers helped people to discover how much fun it could be to create both attractive and useful combinations of herb plantings.

Maggie Oster, too, grew up gardening and cooking. Family meals centered on the joy of seasonal foods, and vacations around the

A mixture of culinary herbs and annual flowers in containers provides a kaleidoscope of flavor and color.

country introduced her to other ingredients and cuisines. With degrees in horticulture and a love of words and photography, she chose to direct her predilections toward publishing. It was in graduate school at Cornell University, with its Robison Herb Garden, that her herbal epiphany occurred. Later, as editor of an indoor and container-gardening magazine based in Seattle, Washington, she gained in-depth practice with this aspect of gardening. A move to New York meant even more experience with small space and container gardening. Both cities and further travel also provided inspiration and further work with foods and cooking. Her interest in edible landscaping has meant trying dozens upon dozens of different fruits, vegetables, and herbs in her various gardens over the years.

About the Recipes

As to the recipes we've included, any cookbook is necessarily arbitrary. Turn us loose tomorrow and we would come up with an entirely different set of recipes. What we hope to accomplish here is to show a range of ideas using fresh herbs that run the gamut from appetizers to salads, soups, main courses, vegetables, grains, beans, breads, desserts, and beverages — as well as some of the condiments, cooking ingredients, and foods that can be flavored with herbs.

The recipes focus on fresh ingredients that can be easily grown in the garden or found in supermarkets. In general, the recipes reflect a healthful approach to eating. Thus, when you want to make egg-rich crème brûlée on a rare occasion, you won't be jeopardizing the health of your arteries.

Our goal is to inspire you to use fresh herbs in all aspects of your cooking every day. Incorporating herbs offers a nutritious, low-calorie way to make food taste better and look better. As we cut down on fats in our diets and eat more vegetables, fruits, and grains, the role of herbs can be important in making these foods even more of a pleasure to cook and serve.

What is most difficult for two confirmed herb lovers to comprehend is why anyone would not use herbs, with all their wonderful fragrances and flavors, in every possible way.

We urge you to be brave and experiment. Only with practice will it become second nature to know what a certain herb tastes like, how it will combine with other ingredients, how cooking or marinating or steeping will change it. Only occasionally should herbs dominate a dish; rather, they add a subtlety of flavor that enhances the other flavors of the dish. Until you become comfortable with herbs, use small amounts. With experience, you'll soon know which herbs in what quantity you and your family enjoy.

Starting a Meal with Herbs

With appetizers — whether snacks, nibbles, or formal first courses — herbs are a quick and easy way to turn the ordinary into the special. For example, simply mince some fresh herbs and add them to a store-bought dip or your favorite recipe. Be sure to try the eggplant dip with marjoram and the black olive spread with garlic chives and thyme that showcase these herbs. Bruschetta or pita crisps take hardly any time to make; adding herbs gives the plain breads luscious flavor. Herb cheeses, toasted nuts with herbs, shallots with tarragon, or herb-marinated olives or goat cheese can be kept on hand for use at a moment's notice. For special occasions try gravlax with dill, fennel, and mint, or low-fat spring rolls flavored exotically with herbs.

Adding fresh herbs and edible flowers, with their attendant flavor and color, to a basic tossed salad puts it on a par with those served at the finest restaurants. Give more depth of flavor to salads by using herbs in salad dressings as well as in the vinegars and oils used to make them. Besides green salads, look to other vegetables and the herbs that can go with them. Try shredded carrots with that hyssop you never knew how to use, or chervil with endive and pears. Even mundane coleslaw takes on a new dimension with fresh caraway leaves. Let the buds of the increasingly popular perennial daylily add crunch to a chicken salad. Cucumber-flavored borage or burnet transforms fennel and radishes, or any salad, without the usual embarrassing side effects of cucumbers.

Soups made "from scratch," whether served steaming on the coldest day of winter or chilled on a sultry summer afternoon, are always one of life's great comfort foods. Fresh herbs improve any soup, be it made from sun-warmed tomatoes scented with tarragon, juicy blueberries with mint and lavender, slow-cooked black beans with thyme and savory, or lentils redolent with sage. Homemade soup takes on a different character when based on low-fat vegetable stock enriched with herbs. Make a large batch and keep containers in the freezer for use on short notice. When you can manage no more than opening a store-bought can of soup, stir in some freshly minced herbs to give it just-made flavor. Whatever the soup, homemade herb crackers or breads embellish the meal.

Herbs in the Main Course

Vegetarian pastas have become the quick-fix health food of the 1990s, and nothing matches them as perfectly as fresh herbs. What could provide instant gratification better than an uncooked tomato sauce brimming with basil? But why stop there? Why not pasta with grilled eggplant and tomatoes? Or a sauce of melon with parsley and

*Cut herbs just as the dew does dry,
Tie them loosely and hang them high.
If you plant to store away,
Stir the leaves a bit each day.*

— Unknown, American Farmer

Recipes pictured: *Rotelle with Eggplant, Tomato, Purple Basil, and Oregano (served over fettucine), Green Bean Salad with Shallots and Mint, Focaccia with Fresh Herbs, and Poached Pears with Sage and Cinnamon Crème Fraîche.*

mint, or arugula with parsley and thyme; a peanut sauce with anise basil, cilantro, and chives; or a pungent black olive and oregano sauce? Or an extra-nutritious meal of whole grain pasta, beans, and greens?

Just about any herb can be used in vegetarian dishes made with eggs, be it quiches (such as one with leeks, thyme, and lavender) or omelets (perhaps with hot peppers and sage). Do you like Tex-Mex food? Use beans cooked with herbs to fill hearty enchiladas or burritos. Quick-cooking tofu, marinated or stir-fried, absorbs the essence of Asian herbs such as ginger, cilantro, anise or lemon basil, and garlic chives. And don't forget to add fresh herbs with lettuce on sandwiches, or to flavor the sandwich fillings with herbs.

Grilled, braised, poached, or baked, the plethora of fish and other seafoods offers a wide range of opportunities to use herbs. Marinades and cooking liquids are the obvious first choices, but try stuffing whole fish with herbs or making spicy seafood stews. The natural affinity of fish and seafood with lemon makes sorrel, lemon basil, lemon thyme, lemongrass, lemon balm, and lemon verbena logical partners. Anise and other herbs that have a licorice flavor, such as fennel, tarragon, and chervil, also blend beautifully with fish and seafood. But don't be afraid to try rosemary, parsley, burnet, or even mint! Be sure to use herb-flavored mustards and butters, too.

Besides medicinal uses, much of the reason for utilizing herbs since ancient times was to hide spoilage in meat. Fortunately that is no longer a concern; now the benefits of mixing herbs and meats are purely those of creating interesting combinations for marinades, sauces, and rubs. Malleable chicken takes to almost every herb flavor, from delicate chervil to robust garlic. Pork also goes well with a wide variety of herbs. Beef is usually best with the heartier herbs, such as oregano, thyme, bay, rosemary, horseradish, and parsley. Lamb and rosemary or mint are inseparable partners, but these are by no means the only choices.

Herbs in Other Dishes

For vitamins, minerals, fiber, and range of flavors, no other food compares with vegetables. Arguably at their best when simply prepared, whether steamed, sautéed, or roasted, vegetables provide limitless ways to utilize herbs. What could be more splendid and gratifying than summer squash, bell peppers, and onions sautéed with a handful of just-picked basil, marjoram, parsley, and garlic chives? Or steamed carrots glazed with honey and mint, rosemary, hyssop, or dill? Do you like your vegetables grilled? For a delicate flavor, use the woody stems of rosemary for skewers. If you don't mind the calories, brush steamed vegetables with an herb-flavored butter. More elaborate vegetable dishes benefit from herbs as well, be it a gratin of fennel and lovage or creamy timbales of carrots, turnips, and rosemary. Adding herbs to beans, grains, and rice turns these nutritious foods into extraordinary fare as well. By varying the herbs used, you can readily change a dish's nationality, matching it to the rest of the meal or your mood.

Special recipes for breads with herbs seem almost unnecessary, for there can't be a basic bread recipe that won't benefit from the addition of herbs. And nothing is as soul-satisfying as the taste and aroma of homemade breads. Treat yourself well and try an easily prepared, no-knead batter yeast bread with rosemary and olives or lemon thyme, a quick bread with herbs and ricotta, or muffins aromatic with chives, shallots, and garlic chives. Flatbreads needn't be plain either, be it a focaccia with Italian herbs or an Indian-influenced bread made with chickpea flour, garlic chives, cilantro, and ginger. Those with a sweet tooth should consider adding mint, clove pinks, lemon verbena, lavender, or cinnamon basil to bread and muffin batters. But even such pungent herbs as sage, rosemary, and thyme can be used with fruits in sweet breads.

Generally, spices are the flavoring of choice for desserts, yet who would not savor a peach and lavender tart, a lemon verbena crème brûlée, or a strawberry-rhubarb crunch with rose geranium? In learning to use herbs in desserts, first consider those with a sweet flavor. These include angelica, anise, anise hyssop, anise basil, cinnamon basil, lemon basil, bergamot, calendula, caraway, ginger, hyssop, lavender, lemon balm, mints, rose, rose geranium, rosemary, and violets. To add extra flavor to desserts, cook or bake with honey or sugar flavored with herbs. And don't forget to garnish with edible flowers, either fresh or crystallized!

Relaxing with a soothing cup of herbal tea evokes the simplicity of using herbs in a wide variety of liquid refreshments. Start your morning with a fruit protein shake made with lemon balm, or use a mocha-mint-cappuccino shake as a great afternoon pick-me-up. For a summer evening soiree, serve a red wine cooler with lemon balm and lemon thyme. For a bridal shower or other party, consider a lavender-basil punch or herb-tea punch. Winter nights call out for mulled herbal cider or cranberry punch with lavender and rosemary. For an intimate after-dinner tête-à-tête, snuggle up with a homemade akavit or other herbal liqueur.

Grow Your Own Fresh Herbs

For those who live in colder climates or with little space or time to garden, having fresh herbs for much of the year may seem an

Be innovative in displaying container-grown herbs. Here an antique wheelbarrow showcases pots of exuberant herbs.

impossibility, but we'll show you how. Easy-to-follow information on growing herbs in containers outdoors is at the core of the gardening section of this book, but there's also information about extending the growing season and raising herbs indoors. You may not have every herb you want year-round, but you'll certainly have enough for culinary inspiration, even on the coldest of days.

A wide selection of herbs can be grown in a small space, and almost all herbs readily adapt to containers. Even if you have a large garden, growing herbs in containers has advantages. The most obvious is that the herbs can be available near your kitchen. It's also fun to have them next to the grill. Or, perhaps set a pot directly under a bedroom or office window, where the fragrances can waft inside. These containers need not be hidden, because the herbs' lush growth and edible flowers are attractive. Place them near the entrance to the house or on the deck, terrace, or patio.

Small pots of herbs can be moved about so they have the best possible sunlight, allowing you to enjoy herbs even when the rest of the garden is shady. For larger containers, place them on a dolly with wheels to gain easy mobility. Growing herbs in containers is great for gardeners with back problems or other disabilities, too. Access, adjustable height, and no weeding or cultivating chores certainly are benefits.

We would be leading you astray to say that growing herbs indoors is as simple as growing a philodendron. But with the guidelines we give on pages 142 to 161 for providing the right conditions, fresh herbs can be yours even if it's snowing outside or if your home has no outside space. The only condition is that your expectations be realistic. The most successful methods involve special artificial light setups. A simple, old-fashioned technique for raising low-growing, hardy herbs in winter is to use a cold frame, as described on page 150.

More than any other group of plants, herbs touch our spirits. They are plants of the senses, calling to us with their scents, colors, flavors, and textures. Sipping a cup of mint tea, savoring a stew perfumed with rosemary, breaking a loaf of bread moist with sage — these link us with people throughout history and from every continent. Cultivating herbs and the herbal palate provides a continuity with our ancestors and all people, enriching our lives with the simple pleasures of the earth and table.

Gravlax with Dill, Fennel, and Mint (page 8) ▶

Appetizers

Gravlax with Dill, Fennel, and Mint

❖

Tart, pungent dill is the Swedish herb of choice for this salt-and-sugar cured salmon, but fennel's anise flavor and the invigorating taste of spearmint work wonderfully, too. Be sure to use the freshest, best quality salmon available.

¼ **cup kosher, or coarse, salt**
¼ **cup sugar**
 1 **teaspoon ground white pepper**
 2 **matching salmon fillets, about 2 pounds each,**
   with pinbones removed but skin left on
⅓ **cup minced fresh dill leaves**
⅓ **cup minced fresh fennel leaves**
⅓ **cup minced fresh spearmint leaves**

Combine the salt, sugar, and white pepper in a small bowl. Cut each salmon fillet into three equal portions and match them, side by side. Cover the skinless side of one pair with the dill, another pair with the fennel, and the third pair with the mint. Sprinkle the salt mixture evenly over all the salmon pieces. Cover three of the pieces with their matching pieces, skinless sides together. Wrap each pair tightly with plastic wrap.

Place each wrapped salmon pair in a separate dish or casserole, cover with a flat board or pan, and weigh down with a brick or several large cans of food. Refrigerate.

Every 12 hours, turn the fillets. They are ready after 48 hours. To serve, scrape the herb mix off each piece and thinly slice at an angle with a long, sharp knife. Serve with thin rye or wheat bread and sliced cucumbers. If desired, garnish with tiny sprigs of fresh herbs.
Yield: 25 to 30 servings

Dill

NATIVE TO PARTS of Europe and Asia, dill has been savored for centuries and is considered both a good luck symbol and a hindrance to witches. The common name is taken from the Norse *dilla*, "to lull," a reference to its calming quality.

The feathery foliage of dill provides a lovely landscape effect. The variety 'Fern Leaf' is especially good for container gardening, as it grows to a compact 18 to 24 inches tall with lots of side branches. Begin harvesting side branches and leaves when plants reach 10 or 12 inches.

Dill leaves and flowers are best when used fresh. Use the seeds either fresh or dried.

BURNET DIP

❖

The cucumber flavor of burnet leaves serves as an admirable replacement for cucumber itself in this dip, which has its origins in several traditional Middle Eastern dishes. Experiment with various kinds of mint to discover your favorite. Sour cream will yield a thicker, richer-tasting dip, whereas the yogurt has a thinner consistency and tarter flavor.

  1 cup fresh burnet leaves
  ¼ cup fresh mint leaves
  1 tablespoon lemon juice
  ¼ teaspoon salt
  1 cup low-fat or nonfat sour cream or plain nonfat yogurt
  ¼ teaspoon ground black pepper

Pulverize the burnet, mint, lemon juice, and salt in a food processor or mortar and pestle. When smooth and of uniform consistency, pour into a bowl and stir in the sour cream or yogurt and the black pepper. Let sit for 1 hour to allow flavors to blend.
Yield: 1⅓ cups

Burnet

HERBED PITA CRISPS

❖

A quick, "homemade" alternative to crackers, pita crisps can be flavored with different oils and herbs. They can be made at the last minute or kept on hand for enjoying at any time.

  Four 6-inch whole wheat pita breads
  ¼ cup extra-virgin olive oil
  2 teaspoons minced fresh rosemary

Heat oven to 275°F. Cut the pita breads into eighths, then open and separate each piece into two. Spread the pieces in a single layer on ungreased baking sheets.
  Combine the olive oil and rosemary in a small bowl. Brush each pita triangle with some of the oil mixture. Bake for 20 to 25 minutes, or until golden and crisp. Let cool before serving, or store in a sealed container, where they will keep for several weeks.
Yield: 32 pita crisps

Vegetable Spring Rolls
with Thai Herbs

························ ❖ ························

The Eastern view of contrasting, or complementary, elements is exemplified in the fusion of the sweet, aromatic peppermint and the tart lemongrass. Black-stem peppermint is an excellent variety for cooking (its rampant growth can be neatly confined in containers). These spring rolls not only are bursting with vegetables, but are also low in fat because they're not deep-fried.

Spring Rolls

- ¾ **pound carrots, shredded**
- ½ **pound Chinese cabbage, shredded**
- 2 **cups bean sprouts**
- 1 **cup minced fresh cilantro leaves**
- ¼ **cup minced fresh peppermint leaves**
- 2 **tablespoons minced fresh lemongrass stalks**
- ¼ **cup minced fresh chives**
- 3 **tablespoons minced fresh gingerroot**
- 5 **tablespoons rice wine vinegar**
- 2 **tablespoons light sesame oil**
- 2 **tablespoons soy sauce**
- 15 **drops hot red pepper sauce**
- ½ **teaspoon five-spice powder**
- ¼ **teaspoon ground cloves**
- 12 **rice paper wrappers**

Dipping Sauce

- ½ **cup lime juice**
- 2 **teaspoons sugar**
- 1 **teaspoon minced fresh cilantro**
- 1 **teaspoon finely chopped roasted unsalted peanuts**
- 1 **teaspoon minced fresh chives**
- 1 **teaspoon fish sauce**
- ½ **teaspoon minced fresh red or green chile pepper**

In a large bowl, combine all ingredients for the spring rolls except the rice paper wrappers. Cover with a plate that just fits inside the bowl, then weigh this down with several bricks, heavy books, or canned goods. After 2 hours, uncover and toss the mixture well. Replace the plate and weights and let sit for another 8 hours.

Uncover bowl and drain off as much liquid as possible. To make the dipping sauce, combine all ingredients in a small bowl and set aside.

To prepare the rice paper wrappers, brush both sides with a pastry brush dipped in hot water, then set aside to soften. Alternatively, use a skillet or large, flat bowl that is slightly larger in diameter than one wrapper. Fill it to within ½ inch of the top with hot water. Immerse a wrapper in the water, then slide a plate underneath to lift it out of the skillet. Pour off any water in the plate and set aside. Wrappers are usually pliable enough to roll in 3 to 5 minutes. With either method, soften one at a time and fill.

To fill a softened wrapper, use ¼ cup of the drained vegetable mixture. Place the mixture to one side of the center. Fold this side over the top of the mixture, then fold in both sides and roll up. Place the seam side down on a serving plate. Cover with a slightly damp towel until all rolls are made. Serve immediately with the dipping sauce.
Yield: 12 spring rolls

RICE PAPER WRAPPERS AND FISH SAUCE

Rice paper wrappers are thin, crisp rounds that must be softened in warm water to make them pliable. Fish sauce, or *nam pla,* is a clear brown salty liquid essential to Thai cooking. Both are available at Asian or Thai groceries or specialty food stores.

Coriander, Cilantro

CILANTRO AND
CHINESE PARSLEY
are two common
names for
Coriandrum sativum,
but the seeds are
referred to as coriander.
The name is a derivation from
the Greek *koris,* meaning "bug."

Early Sanskrit writings and
Egyptian tomb relics from almost
3,000 years ago give evidence of
the use of coriander seeds. These
have been described as having a
flavor combining lemon, sage, and
caraway. Light brown, ribbed, and
about ⅛ inch long, the seeds are
used whole or ground in pickles,
mulled wine, curry and garam
masala blends, soups, sauces, fruit
desserts, and with all types of meat.

The flavor and scent of fresh
coriander leaves is distinctive, to say
the least. As you acquire a taste for
them, you'll come to realize how
essential they are to Mexican,
Turkish, Indian, and Asian cuisine.
Salads, fresh tomato salsa,
guacamole, beans, fried rice, and
stir-fried foods are so much the
better for them. If used in cooked
dishes, add them near the end of
preparation.

WATERCRESS AND STILTON CANAPES

❖

2 ounces Stilton cheese or ¼ cup
    crumbled blue cheese, at room
    temperature
2 tablespoons dry port wine
2 tablespoons low-fat or nonfat
    sour cream
2 ounces low-fat cream cheese
8 slices thin white or wheat
    bread
    Ground black pepper
1½ cups minced watercress or
    garden cress

The English are devoted to the pepper-flavored cresses, be they the moisture-loving watercress (Nasturtium officinale) or quick-growing garden cress (Lepidium sativum) — which reaches harvest-size on a windowsill in just a few weeks. These little sandwiches are part of that British heritage and are perfect for an afternoon tea or twilight garden party.

U sing an electric mixer, cream the Stilton or blue cheese, port, sour cream, and cream cheese. Spread the mixture on the bread and sprinkle with black pepper. Scatter the cress on four of the toast slices, and top with the other four pieces of toast. Cut out small shapes with a cookie cutter, or trim the crusts and cut diagonally into halves, then halve again.
Yield: 32 triangles

BLACK OLIVE SPREAD WITH
GARLIC CHIVES AND THYME

❖

12 ounces drained, pitted black
    olives
1½ cups grated Parmesan cheese
    or fat-free Italian cheese blend
½ cup herb–white wine vinegar
⅓ cup tomato paste
⅓ cup extra–virgin olive oil
½ cup fresh garlic chives
¼ cup fresh thyme or lemon
    thyme leaves

Even people who aren't fond of olives find this spread delectable. Make canapes by spreading it on thin slices of bread cut into triangles or other shapes. It even makes a great meal-sized sandwich; try it with Bibb lettuce on Herb-Ricotta Tomato Quick Bread (see page 110). This recipe has been adapted from one in The St. Louis Herb Society Cookbook.

C ombine all ingredients in a food processor. Refrigerate in a covered container. Variation: Substitute chives for the garlic chives and add 1 clove garlic.
Yield: 2¼ cups

Eggplant Dip with Marjoram and Balsamic Vinegar

◆

Easy to make, this dip may be served with pita or bagel crisps or fresh vegetables cut for dipping. Native to the Mediterranean where this dish has its origins, marjoram has a sweet, delicate oregano-like fragrance and flavor. Try it with a variety of meat, vegetable, and egg dishes. If you've had trouble growing true sweet marjoram (Origanum majorana), try evergreen marjoram (Origanum X majoricum).

2½ **pounds peeled eggplant, cut into ¾-inch cubes**
1½ **tablespoons kosher, or coarse, salt**
⅓ **cup canola oil**
4 **cups chopped yellow onions**
6 **garlic cloves, minced**
2 **tablespoons fresh marjoram leaves**
3 **tablespoons balsamic vinegar**
2 **tablespoons water**
½ **teaspoon ground black pepper**

Marjoram

Put the eggplant cubes in a large strainer or colander and toss them with the salt. Let sit and drain for an hour. Rinse, drain, and dry the eggplant cubes with a towel.

Heat the oven to 350°F. In a large, deep, ovenproof, lidded skillet, heat the oil over medium-high heat. Add the eggplant and cook, stirring, 6 to 7 minutes or until soft. Add the onions, garlic, and marjoram. Cook, stirring, for 5 minutes or until onions soften. Add the vinegar, water, and black pepper. Cover and bake in the oven for 1 hour, adding a bit more water after 30 minutes if the mixture seems too dry. Remove from the oven and let cool completely. Serve cold as a dip or as a side dish to a meal, either heated or at room temperature.
Yield: 4 cups

Eggplant "Belly Buttons"

Whenever possible, choose male eggplants because they have fewer seeds and are less bitter. To determine the difference between male and female, look at the small spot on the bottom where the eggplant was attached to the flower. Female eggplants have a deep, belly button–like indentation, whereas males have a shallow, scar-like spot.

CHERRY TOMATOES STUFFED WITH HERBED FRESH CHEESE

8 ounces farmer's cheese, dry-curd cottage cheese, low-fat cream cheese, low-fat or non-fat ricotta, or homemade non-fat yogurt cheese

2 tablespoons minced fresh parsley leaves

1 tablespoon minced fresh thyme leaves

1 tablespoon minced fresh tarragon leaves

1 tablespoon minced fresh oregano leaves

2 tablespoons lemon juice

½ teaspoon red wine vinegar

¼ teaspoon salt

¼ teaspoon ground black pepper

20 cherry tomatoes

40 fresh miniature basil sprigs
   Balsamic vinegar

Here's the perfect summer party food — low fat, no cooking, colorful, and using a mixture of the easiest-to-grow herbs. If the herbs listed are unavailable, or (heaven forbid!) you don't like some of them, use your own favorite combination. Try any of the various basils, marjoram, or even fresh sage.

Combine cheese, parsley, thyme, tarragon, oregano, lemon juice, vinegar, salt, and pepper in a food processor or mix by hand in a bowl. Cut the tomatoes in half and with a demitasse spoon or small melon baller, scoop out the seeds. Fill each half with a spoonful of the cheese mixture. Garnish with a basil sprig and a drop of balsamic vinegar.

Yield: 40 pieces

The cherry tomato is a marvelous invention, producing as it does a satisfactory explosive squish when bitten.

— Miss Manners

TOMATO AND BASIL TOASTS

These little toasts, or bruschetta in Italian, are the essence of summer with luscious, juicy tomatoes and the sweet, spicy perfume of basil. The layer of roasted garlic lends richness and depth. For a lighter touch, just rub slices with a garlic clove cut in half. Try other cheeses besides this Italian classic, or omit if you're watching calories. Other options include adding or substituting capers, anchovies, or other herbs, such as fennel, chervil, marjoram, or parsley.

Heat the oven broiler. Brush both sides of each slice of bread with the olive oil. Place on an ungreased baking sheet and broil until very lightly toasted, or about 5 minutes.

Spread a thin layer of garlic purée on each slice, then sprinkle on some tomatoes, basil, salt and pepper to taste, and cheese. Return to the oven and bake about 5 minutes, or until the cheese is melted. Serve immediately.

Yield: 16 pieces

1 thin baguette French bread about 16 inches long, cut on the diagonal into ¾-inch slices
Extra-virgin olive oil
¼ cup Roasted Garlic Purée (see recipe)
1 pound tomatoes, peeled, seeded, and chopped
¼ cup minced fresh basil leaves
Salt and freshly ground black pepper to taste
4 ounces fontina cheese, shredded

ROASTED GARLIC PURÉE

What slowly baked garlic loses in bite it gains in rich sweetness. Its soft, spreadable consistency makes it a useful ingredient to have on hand. Besides its traditional use on slices of toasted Italian bread, try it in mashed potatoes, sauces, salad dressings, mayonnaise, soups, stews, flavored butters, or whenever fresh garlic is required. Make enough to have some immediately, plus leftovers to store refrigerated in a jar for up to 1 month.

Heat oven to 300°F. Slice the top from the head of garlic. Remove most of the papery outer skin without allowing the cloves to separate. Place in a small ovenproof dish or terracotta garlic roaster.

Pour olive oil and brandy or balsamic vinegar over the top. A sprig of rosemary may also be added to the dish. Cover dish with aluminum foil or a lid and bake about 1 hour, or until tender. Remove from the oven. When cool, squeeze the garlic from the skins and mash.

A somewhat milder version is possible by poaching the garlic briefly in milk before roasting. Place the prepared head of garlic upside down in a saucepan, cover with milk, and simmer over low heat for 10 minutes. Drain and rinse under cold running water. Then place in a small baking dish and bake as directed.

1 head garlic
1 tablespoon extra-virgin olive oil
1 tablespoon brandy or balsamic vinegar

GRILLED PORTOBELLO MUSHROOMS AND TOMATOES WITH HERBED GOAT CHEESE

❖

4 ounces fresh goat cheese
1 tablespoon minced fresh basil leaves
1 tablespoon minced fresh marjoram leaves
1 tablespoon minced fresh chives
2 tablespoons olive oil
   Four 2-ounce portobello mushrooms, stems removed and caps wiped clean
   Four ¾-inch slices fresh tomatoes (approximately the same diameter as the mushrooms or slightly smaller)
   Salt and freshly ground black pepper to taste

Smokey, sumptuous portobello mushrooms combined with juicy tomatoes and tart goat cheese accented with the flavors and scent of herbs yields an elegant meatless appetizer.

In a small bowl, stir together cheese, basil, marjoram, and chives. Prepare grill or heat the oven broiler. Brush olive oil on both sides of each mushroom and tomato slice. Grill or broil mushrooms and tomatoes 2 to 3 minutes per side, or until tender and golden. Season with salt and pepper. Put a tomato slice on each mushroom, then spread with the cheese mixture. Return to grill or broiler and cook until cheese melts. Serve immediately.
Yield: 4 servings

HERB CHEESE

8 ounces fresh cheese
1 garlic clove, minced
¼ cup minced fresh herb leaves

You can make your own savory blend of herb cheese from your favorite blend of cheese and herbs. Depending on your inclination, you can use regular or light cream cheese; regular, low-fat, or nonfat ricotta; fresh goat cheese; or homemade nonfat yogurt cheese.

For herbs, almost any can be used alone or in infinite combinations. Also consider adding minced olives or finely chopped toasted nuts. Even "sweet" herbs such as mint, angelica, or sweet cicely can be used, perhaps with the addition of some fruit preserves or unsweetened fresh fruit and herb-flavored honey. Don't forget about edible flowers, either. Try nasturtium flowers and leaves, anise hyssop, violas, or pinks with cinnamon and honey.

The obvious use of herb cheese is as a serve-yourself spread. Or, spread it on thin bread as a canapé. Or, fill tartlet or phyllo shells and bake briefly. Herb cheese also serves as a filling for omelets, crepes, and ravioli.

By hand or in a food processor, combine all ingredients until well blended. If cheese is too thick, add a bit of cream or milk until of desired consistency. Store in an airtight container in the refrigerator, allowing flavors to blend for at least a day before serving.
Yield: About 1 cup

Chives

CHIVES ARE ONE OF the staples of the herbal repertoire. Their delicate, onion-like flavor enlivens just about any dish that isn't sweet — including salads, egg and cheese dishes, herb cheese, sauces, vegetables, meat, poultry, fish, and breads.

Chives contain significant amounts of vitamins A and C, thiamine, and niacin, as well as iron, calcium, magnesium, phosphorus, and potassium.

Separate the mauve-colored flowers of chives into individual florets when using as a garnish or adding to salads, herb cheese, or tea sandwiches. Use whole flowers to flavor and color vinegar.

Add chives in the last few minutes of cooking to avoid destroying their flavor.

SWEET-AND-SOUR TARRAGON SHALLOTS

Shallots

With a mild flavor often described as being a cross between onion and garlic, shallots are exceedingly versatile in the kitchen. The delightful morsels in this recipe utilize shallots that may be too small for other purposes. Besides serving them as part of an appetizer selection, use them as an accompaniment to roasted or grilled meats. Pearl onions may be substituted for the shallots.

1 pound small shallots, unpeeled
2 tablespoons extra-virgin olive oil
½ cup tarragon–white wine vinegar
2 tablespoons sugar
1 tablespoon minced fresh tarragon leaves
½ teaspoon salt
¼ teaspoon ground black pepper

Bring a large saucepan of water to a boil over medium-high heat. Add the shallots, bring back to a boil, and cook 5 minutes. Drain the shallots and rinse with cold water. When cool enough to handle, trim off the root and tip ends and peel.

In a large skillet, heat the oil over medium heat. Add the shallots and cook, stirring frequently, for 10 minutes or until beginning to soften. Stir in the vinegar, sugar, tarragon, salt, and pepper. Reduce heat to low, cover, and cook about 10 minutes, stirring occasionally, or until shallots are tender. Serve warm or at room temperature.
Yield: 6 servings

COOKING WITH SHALLOTS

Shallots are mild enough to be used uncooked in salads or, when cooked, in any dish that would be enhanced with a delicate onion flavor. Most often, shallots are used to flavor fish, quiche, soups, sauces, and butters. Take care that shallots do not brown while cooking, as this turns them bitter.

TOASTED NUTS WITH HERBS

❖

Great nibbles to keep on hand for enjoying by yourself as a snack or serving as part of a tea table or cocktail buffet, herb-flavored nuts can be made with a variety of herbs. Experiment, too, with different nuts, either one kind or in combination.

1 large egg white
¼ cup sugar
1 tablespoon water
¼ cup minced fresh herb leaves
½ teaspoon salt
1 pound pecans, walnuts, Brazil nuts, hazelnuts, or pistachios

Heat oven to 225°F. In a medium-sized bowl, beat egg white with sugar and water until foamy. Add the herbs and salt, blending well. Stir in nuts, coating thoroughly. Spread nuts in a single layer on one or more parchment-covered or nonstick baking sheets. Bake 1 hour, stirring every 15 minutes. Cool and store in an airtight container in the refrigerator.
Yield: About 4 cups

HERB-MARINATED GOAT CHEESE

❖

Until recently only French goat cheese, or chevre, was available. Now there are a number of excellent domestic brands offered by small producers. Adaptable to many cooking uses, fresh goat cheese may be best appreciated as an appetizer or snack when simply marinated with herbs — especially basil, thyme, rosemary, marjoram, chives, or fennel. Use both fresh leaves and flowers for the marinade and as a garnish.

8 ounces fresh goat cheese
2 tablespoons whole or coarsely chopped fresh herb leaves or edible flowers
10 whole black, green, or white peppercorns
Extra-virgin olive oil

Cut cheese into ½-inch-thick slices. In a glass jar, layer slices with herbs and peppercorns. Cover with olive oil and attach the lid. Let sit for at least a day to allow flavors to blend. This will stay fresh for about a week at room temperature. If desired, store in the refrigerator, bringing to room temperature before serving.
Yield: 8 ounces

HERB-MARINATED OLIVES

❖

SEASONING CHOICES

1 bay leaf
1 or more red or green chile
  peppers
1 teaspoon whole black, green, or
  white peppercorns; allspice
  berries; or mustard, fennel,
  coriander, or cardamom seeds
3 or more garlic cloves, thinly
  sliced
  Zest of 1 orange or lemon
1 lemon, cut into 6 wedges
½ cup whole or coarsely chopped
  herbs, such as fresh anise,
  rosemary, basil, cilantro,
  fennel, marjoram, oregano,
  or thyme

Whether you choose the basic canned variety or from among the many wonderful imported types, olives are transformed when marinated with herbs and either lemon juice or olive oil. New olives may be added to the jar as they are used up. Just be sure to keep them covered with the marinade. Or, use the flavored oil in salads or other marinades. Don't panic when the olive oil congeals in the refrigerator; it quickly returns to liquid at room temperature. Marinated olives will keep in the refrigerator for 6 months.

Herbs and other seasonings can be combined in innumerable ways for flavoring olives. For every 1 pound of olives, choose from among the ingredients listed.

To prepare 1 pound of olives with lemon juice, drain the olives, reserving the brine. Layer olives with herbs and other seasonings of choice in a glass jar. Pour ¾ cup lemon juice and ¼ cup vinegar, preferably lemon-flavored, over the olives. Add enough reserved brine to cover, and attach the lid. Refrigerate for several days before using.

To prepare 1 pound of olives with olive oil, drain the olives, discarding the brine. Layer olives with herbs and other seasonings of choice in a glass jar. Pour extra-virgin olive oil over the olives to cover. Attach the lid and refrigerate for several days before using. *Yield: 1 pound*

SALAD OILS

Olive oil. The extra-virgin olive oil is the oil of choice. The best ones are made from hand-picked olives and are cold-pressed. There is a great range of flavors and colors, with the oils from Spain, Greece, and southern Italy being the strongest and those from Tuscany and Provence being lighter. Olive oil is monounsaturated, which is best for reducing blood cholesterol.

Nut oils. Oils made from walnuts and hazelnuts have a rich flavor and scent. They pair well with fruit or sherry vinegars. They are delicate and turn rancid quickly, so are best kept refrigerated after opening. Polyunsaturated.

Almond oil. This oil is light and slightly sweet. Pair it with a light vinegar and delicate greens. High in monounsaturates.

Sesame oil. Light, cold-pressed sesame oil has a light, nutty flavor, good on salads or in cooking. Intensely flavored dark sesame oil, made from toasted sesame seeds, is used mainly for salads, pairing well with red wine vinegars, or added as a last-minute flavoring to stir-fries. Polyunsaturated.

Canola oil. Light in color, with little flavor, and monounsaturated, this is an excellent all-purpose oil for salads and cooking.

*What was Paradise?
but a Garden,
an Orchard of Trees
and Herbs, full of pleasure,
and nothing there but
delights . . .*

— William Lawson

Asparagus with Yellow Tomato and Herb Concassée (page 22) ▶

Salads

Asparagus with Yellow Tomato and Herb Concassée

.... ❖ ....

The tonality of anise, derived from the chervil and tarragon, is counterpointed with savory's quality of thyme and mint in this fresh tomato dressing for lightly cooked asparagus. This combination is a variation of the classic mixture fines herbes, which variously includes chives, parsley, burnet, marjoram, or watercress. Each of these herbs is at its best when used uncooked or added just at the end of cooking.

1 pound yellow tomatoes, peeled, seeded, and chopped
⅓ cup extra-virgin olive oil
2 tablespoons white wine or rice vinegar
1 teaspoon chopped fresh chervil leaves
1 teaspoon chopped fresh savory leaves
1 teaspoon chopped fresh tarragon leaves
½ teaspoon salt
¼ teaspoon ground black pepper
1½ pounds asparagus spears, each about ⅜- to ½-inch in diameter
¾ pound Bibb lettuce
⅓ cup tarragon oil

Combine the tomatoes, olive oil, vinegar, chervil, savory, tarragon, salt, and pepper in a bowl and let sit for 1 hour to allow flavors to blend.

Trim the ends of the asparagus so that all spears are about 6 inches long. In an asparagus steamer or a large covered saucepan fitted with a collapsible vegetable steamer, bring 1 inch of water to a boil. Steam the asparagus for 1½ minutes, then plunge it into ice water to stop the cooking. Drain and chill, wrapped in a towel. Toss the asparagus and lettuce gently with the tarragon oil, then divide and lay the lettuce out on four plates. Top with the asparagus, then with a crown of the tomato-herb mixture.

Yield: 4 servings

Tarragon Oil

Tarragon oil is available at specialty stores. Alternatively, substitute ¼ cup extra-virgin olive oil and 1 tablespoon minced fresh tarragon leaves.

Chervil brings out the best in other herbs and foods with which it is combined, just as some charming people stimulate others about them.

— Mary Mason Campbell, *Kitchen Gardens*

CARROT SALAD WITH BLACK OLIVES AND HYSSOP

❖

A member of the Mint Family, hyssop has a slightly bitter flavor with an undertone of mint. It especially complements salads and fruit dishes, but the intriguing flavor is also good with soups and stews. A beautiful garden plant, hyssop has lovely edible blue flowers that attract butterflies. If desired, mint may be substituted for hyssop.

½ pound carrots, shredded (about 2½ cups)
½ cup pitted, chopped black olives
1½ tablespoons extra-virgin olive oil
2 tablespoons minced fresh hyssop leaves
1 tablespoon balsamic vinegar
1 tablespoon white wine or rice vinegar
¼ teaspoon ground black pepper

Combine all ingredients in a bowl and toss. Cover and refrigerate for at least 2 hours to allow flavors to blend. Garnish with fresh hyssop blossoms, if available.

Yield: 4 servings

VINEGARS

The earliest written records of vinegar are from about 7,000 years ago. Vinegar naturally occurs when certain bacteria come into contact with wine or other fermented liquids and oxygen. Long serving as a medicine and a preservative, vinegar is now mainly used for pickling, in salad dressings, and as a low-calorie enhancement for other foods.

Distilled vinegar. Made from grain or other substances, colorless and among the harshest flavored. Mainly used for pickling.

Cider vinegar. Made from apples, golden in color, with a strong, fruity flavor that intensifies with cooking. For salad dressing, it best complements strongly flavored greens and smoked fish or meat.

Wine vinegar. The most common include red, white, wine, champagne, and sherry. Preferred because it is not harsh, has excellent flavor, and is very versatile. Sherry vinegar is particularly smooth from aging in wooden casks.

Rice vinegar. From China, Japan, and other Asian countries. Different types vary greatly; Japanese are usually the most mellow.

Malt vinegar. Made from ale, with a robust, yeasty flavor.

Balsamic vinegar. The true product is made in Modena, Italy, from the unfermented juice of sweet grapes that has been boiled to a syrup and aged for years in wooden casks. The intense flavor is both tart and sweet. Needless to say, it is also very expensive. Balsamic vinegar from the average grocery is a manufactured product. To improve the flavor of inexpensive balsamic vinegar, stir 1 teaspoon of melted dark brown sugar into 1 cup of balsamic vinegar.

GREEN BEAN SALAD WITH SHALLOTS AND MINT

❖

1 pound fresh green beans
½ cup chopped, toasted walnuts
½ cup coarsely chopped fresh
    mint leaves
½ cup minced shallots
2 tablespoons white wine or
    rice vinegar
½ teaspoon salt
¼ teaspoon ground black pepper
¼ cup walnut oil
2 tablespoons extra-virgin
    olive oil

With over 600 varieties of mint available, choosing just a few kinds to grow may seem insurmountable. For both beauty and intense peppermint flavor, 'Blue Balsam' mint is favored. Others to consider are Mentha spicata 'Crispata', with its sharp, clean aroma and dark, curly leaves. Mentha spicata 'Crispii' is similar, but the leaves are smaller and even more densely curled.

Trim the ends from the beans, remove strings if necessary, and break into 2-inch pieces. In a large covered saucepan fitted with a collapsible vegetable steamer, bring 1 inch of water to a boil. Add the beans, cover, and cook for 5 to 6 minutes, or until they are tender but still crisp. Rinse immediately under cold water and pat dry with a towel. Put them in a bowl with the walnuts.

To make the dressing, whisk the mint, shallots, vinegar, salt, and pepper in a small bowl. Slowly add the walnut and olive oils, whisking continuously. Pour the dressing over the beans and gently toss. Cover and let sit for 30 minutes to allow flavors to blend. Serve immediately or refrigerate before serving.
Yield: 6 servings

Mint I grow in abundance and in all its varieties. How many there are, I might as well try to count the sparks from Vulcan's furnace beneath Etna.

— Abbot Walafrid Strabo

Endive, Pear, and Chervil Salad

❖❖

The delicate, feathery leaves of chervil, with their whisper of anise, are almost never found in stores. Fortunately, they are easily grown at home, albeit they are at their best in spring and fall when the weather is cooler. They quickly go to seed, so start a new pot every four weeks for a continuous supply. The seventeenth-century herbalist John Evelyn has written, "The tender tips of chervil should never be wanting in our sallets, being exceedingly wholesome and cheering of the spirits."

C ombine the water and lemon juice in a bowl. Peel and core the pears and cut in wedges ¼-inch thick. Put the slices in the lemon water to prevent browning.

In a large bowl, combine the vinegar, grapefruit juice, and pepper. Slowly whisk in the canola and walnut oils, pouring them in a thin stream. Drain the pears and gently toss with the vinaigrette. Tear the escarole and chervil into bite-sized pieces. Add these and the chives to the pears and toss carefully but thoroughly.

Yield: 6 to 8 servings

- 1 cup cold water
- 1 tablespoon lemon juice
- ½ pound fresh pears
- 1 tablespoon white wine or champagne vinegar
- ½ tablespoon grapefruit juice
- ¼ teaspoon ground black pepper
- 2 tablespoons canola oil
- 1 tablespoon walnut oil
- 1 pound escarole, cored, washed, and dried
- 1 cup fresh chervil leaves
- ¼ cup minced fresh chives

Basic Vinaigrette

Endless variations are possible on the basic salad dressing composed of oil, vinegar, and herbs. Try different salad oils, vinegars, and mustards, including flavored ones. A single herb or a mixture. Experiment, experiment, experiment! Don't be afraid to add herbs to a favorite recipe or other recipes that sound intriguing.

At one time the basic proportions for an oil-and-vinegar dressing were 4 parts oil to 1 part vinegar, but with the concern over fat consumption, most people use less oil now, or 2 to 3 parts oil. For a low-fat version, substitute de-fatted stock or broth, carrot juice, buttermilk, nonfat yogurt, or low-fat tofu for the oil.

Combine vinegar, herbs, lemon juice, mustard, salt, and black pepper in a small bowl. Add ½ teaspoon honey or 1 minced garlic clove, if desired. Slowly add olive oil in a thin stream, whisking continuously. Use immediately or store in the refrigerator for up to 3 weeks, shaking well before serving.

Yield: ¾ cup

- ¼ cup vinegar
- 1 to 4 teaspoons minced fresh herbs
- 1 to 2 teaspoons lemon juice
- 1 to 2 teaspoons prepared mustard
- ½ teaspoon salt
- ¼ to ½ teaspoon freshly ground pepper
- ½ teaspoon honey (optional)
- 1 garlic clove, minced (optional)
- ½ cup extra-virgin olive oil (or other oil)

ROASTED PEPPER, FRESH MOZZARELLA, AND BASIL SALAD

* * *

½ **pound fresh mozzarella**
5 **tablespoons extra-virgin olive oil**
3 **garlic cloves, peeled and crushed**
2 **tablespoons minced fresh thyme leaves**
2 **tablespoons minced fresh oregano leaves**
  Minced zest of 1 lemon (2 to 3 teaspoons)
4 **medium red bell peppers**
4 **medium yellow bell peppers**
1 **cup fresh basil leaves**
2 **tablespoons small capers, drained**
2 **tablespoons balsamic vinegar**
¼ **teaspoon ground black pepper**
  Fresh basil flowers (optional)

Bearing the perfume and flavors of the Mediterranean kitchen, this robust salad is filling enough to serve as a meal in itself with plump loaves of crusty bread. Experiment with different basil varieties or use a mixture: perhaps some intense, haunting 'Genoa Green Improved' (also called 'Genovese') and richly mellow 'Neapolitano'. Oreganos are extremely variable in flavor, but usually the best is labeled "Greek."

Cut the mozzarella into 1-inch pieces or use a melon baller to make 1-inch spheres. Alternatively, you may be able to find *bocconcini*, which are little balls of freshly made mozzarella. Combine the mozzarella with 3 tablespoons of the olive oil, garlic, thyme, oregano, and lemon zest. Marinate at room temperature for at least 1 hour.

Under a broiler or on a grill, roast the peppers, turning them as each side blackens. When the peppers are blackened all over, put them in a paper bag or lidded container to steam. When they have cooled, peel off the skin, scrape out the seeds, and cut the peeled pepper into inch-wide strips.

Combine the peppers, basil, capers, balsamic vinegar, the remaining 2 tablespoons of olive oil, black pepper, and the marinade from the mozzarella in a large bowl and toss. On a serving platter or individual plates, arrange the peppers and basil leaves in a contrasting color pattern. Top the leaves with the mozzarella, then pour any remaining dressing over the platter. Garnish with fresh basil flowers, if desired.

Yield: 8 salad or 4 main-course servings

Basil

BASIL HAS A SWEET, spicy flavor and scent with a wide-ranging affinity to all manner of foods. Basil is best known for its use in Italian and other Mediterranean cuisines, especially with tomatoes and cheese. Besides pesto, pasta, and pizza, consider basil with meat, seafood, poultry, and vegetables, and in soups, salads, breads, muffins, egg dishes, polenta, rice, flavored butters, tomato and vegetable juices, and fruit desserts. Be sure to flavor some white and red wine vinegars with different varieties of basil.

Because it loses much of its flavor when dried, basil is better frozen. One way to prepare it is to dip whole stems in boiling water for a few seconds, then immediately dip in ice water. Strip the leaves from the stem, pat them dry, and freeze in a single layer on a tray. Store frozen leaves in an airtight plastic bag. Another way is to purée the leaves with a little water in a blender, then pour the mixture into ice cube trays, freeze, and store the cubes in freezer bags.

ARUGULA, BEET, AND GOAT CHEESE SALAD

⬧

1½ pounds fresh beets
3 tablespoons white wine or rice vinegar
¼ cup cold water
2 tablespoons canola oil
1 tablespoon walnut oil
6 ounces fresh arugula, washed, dried, and torn into bite-sized pieces (about 3 cups)
4 ounces fresh goat cheese, crumbled into ½-inch chunks
¼ teaspoon ground black pepper

Nutty, slightly bitter, with undertones of mustard and pepper, the flavor of arugula finds its complement in sweet fresh beets. In Mediterranean cuisines, where arugula grows wild, it is often paired with fresh goat or feta cheese as well as fresh citrus, olives, and artichokes.

Heat oven to 375°F. Wash the beets and leave 1 inch of stem. Put the beets in a baking dish or on a cookie sheet and bake for 1 to 2 hours, or until a fork pierces them easily. When cool enough to handle, peel and cut into ½-inch cubes. Put them in a bowl and add 2 tablespoons of the vinegar and the water. Toss and refrigerate for at least 1 hour.

Put the remaining 1 tablespoon vinegar into a large bowl and slowly whisk in the canola and walnut oils, pouring them in a thin stream. Add the arugula, goat cheese, and pepper and gently toss. Divide and arrange this mixture on six plates. Drain the beets and scatter them over the top.
Yield: 6 servings

HERB VINEGAR

2 cups vinegar
1 cup fresh or ½ cup dried herb leaves, seeds, or flowers

Making herb vinegars is as easy as growing the herbs themselves. Just be sure to use a good quality vinegar, be it pure apple cider, white, red, or rice wine, or sherry.

Herb combinations with stronger flavors, such as thyme, oregano, rosemary, and bay are better suited to a red wine vinegar. White and rice wine vinegars are delicate enough not to overpower the "lighter" herbs, such as chives, basil, or tarragon. And some herbs work with any vinegar. Plus, don't forget about spices, hot peppers, garlic, shallots, and ginger.

Use vinegars daily in salad dressings, marinades, for glazing vegetables and meats, sweet-and-sour stir-fries, pickles, and homemade mustards.

Combine the vinegar and herbs (or other ingredients) in a clean quart jar. Be sure all the leaves are submerged. Cover with a non-metal lid or put plastic wrap over the top first if using a metal lid. Store in a cool, dark place for 2 weeks. Check the flavor. Let steep another week or two, if desired. Strain and put into clean small bottles, as desired. Use corks or plastic caps. Store away from strong light, which destroys the flavor.
Yield: 2 cups

FENNEL, RADISH, AND BORAGE SALAD WITH CITRUS VINAIGRETTE

The refreshing cucumber taste of borage adds a delightful flavor to salads. And if you feel slightly disquieted with the world, perhaps the inclusion of borage will also have its traditional effect of lifting the spirits. Your mood most certainly will brighten by tossing in a few of the luminous blue star-shaped flowers.

½ pound bulb fennel
½ cup small, young fresh borage leaves, torn into bite-sized pieces
6 ounces radishes, thinly sliced
1 tablespoon grapefruit juice
1 teaspoon white wine vinegar
½ teaspoon salt
¼ teaspoon ground black pepper
2 tablespoons walnut oil
1 tablespoon canola oil

To prepare the fennel, first cut the top off the fennel and remove any discolored outer portions; then slice the bulb in half from top to bottom, cut out the core, and finally cut thin slices, starting at the bottom. Toss the borage, radishes, and fennel together in a large serving bowl.

In a small bowl, combine the grapefruit juice, vinegar, salt, and pepper. Whisk in the walnut and canola oils, adding them in a thin stream. Toss and serve.

Variation: Substitute fresh burnet leaves for the borage leaves.

Yield: 4 servings

WATERCRESS AND ORANGE SALAD

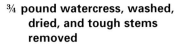

¾ pound watercress, washed,
    dried, and tough stems
    removed
2 medium-size navel oranges
2 ounces Saga cheese, crumbled
¼ cup extra-virgin olive oil
1 tablespoon red wine vinegar
1 teaspoon prepared Dijon-style
    mustard
¼ teaspoon ground black pepper

The lively, peppery taste of watercress and the astringent sweetness of oranges need little embellishment save the best vinegar, olive oil, and the soft-ripened blue cheese called Saga.

Divide the watercress among four salad plates. Prepare each orange by slicing off the top and bottom, then cutting off the rind and outer white membrane. Finally, holding the orange over a bowl to catch the juice, cut the segments apart, removing the white membrane from the sides. Arrange the orange segments over the watercress.

In a small bowl, combine the reserved orange juice, cheese, olive oil, vinegar, mustard, and pepper. Pour the dressing over the salad and serve immediately.
Yield: 4 servings

HERB CROUTONS

Homemade herb croutons make a nice addition to nearly any salad. They are not only simple but much more flavorful than store-bought croutons. The herbs used can be matched to the salad or your individual preferences.

Heat oven to 300°F. Cut the crusts from six slices of bread, and cut the slices into ½-inch cubes. In a large nonstick skillet, heat 2 tablespoons butter and 2 tablespoons canola oil. Mix in 2 teaspoons of crushed dried herbs and 1 minced garlic clove, if desired. Add bread cubes and stir well to coat. Spread the bread cubes in a single layer on a baking sheet. Bake 25 to 30 minutes, or until golden and crisp.

Cool. Store in an airtight container in a cool place.

Potato Salad with Mustard and Herbs

You'll never settle for bland deli potato salad after tasting this version with lots of mustard, onions, pickles, and palate-tingling parsley, dill, and horseradish.

Wash the potatoes and cut into ¾-inch pieces. Cook in boiling salted water about 20 minutes, until tender. Drain and cool. To make the dressing, combine mayonnaise dressing and mustard in a bowl.

Toss the cooled potatoes, dressing, onions, pickles, parsley, dill, horseradish, salt, and pepper together in a large bowl. Cover and refrigerate overnight to allow the flavors to blend.
Yield: 8 servings

2½ **pounds new potatoes (each about 1½ inches in diameter)**
¾ **cup low-fat or reduced-calorie mayonnaise dressing**
2 **tablespoons prepared Dijon-style mustard**
2 **cups chopped sweet onion, such as Vidalia or Walla Walla**
1½ **cups finely chopped sour dill pickles**
½ **cup chopped fresh parsley leaves**
¼ **cup chopped fresh dill leaves**
1 **tablespoon grated horseradish (fresh or preserved in vinegar)**
1 **teaspoon salt**
½ **teaspoon ground black pepper**

Multicolored Coleslaw with Fresh Caraway

Although the seed of caraway is most often used in the kitchen, such as with cooked cabbage, rye bread, or goulash, the aromatic leaves of caraway lend a lighter but still familiar and pleasurable flavor to salads and soups.

In a large bowl, combine all ingredients and toss thoroughly. Cover and refrigerate for at least 8 hours before serving.
Yield: 6 servings

½ **pound red cabbage, coarsely shredded**
½ **pound green cabbage, coarsely shredded**
⅓ **pound carrots, shredded**
¼ **cup minced fresh caraway leaves**
¼ **cup cider vinegar**
2 **tablespoons canola oil**
1 **tablespoon grated fresh gingerroot**
½ **teaspoon salt**
½ **teaspoon ground black pepper**

VEGETABLE-QUINOA SALAD

❖

2 cups water or vegetable broth
1 cup quinoa
1 cup cooked green beans, cut in
   1-inch lengths
½ cup chopped scallions
½ cup chopped, toasted hazelnuts
¼ cup pitted, sliced ripe olives
¼ pound carrots, shredded
1 red bell pepper, cored, seeded,
   and diced
¼ pound summer squash, diced
½ cup chopped fresh basil leaves
½ cup chopped fresh parsley
   leaves
¼ cup chopped fresh burnet
   leaves
¼ cup hazelnut oil
¼ cup white wine or rice vinegar

Quinoa (pronounced "keen-wa") is an ancient grain native to the Andes that, unlike other grains, is a complete protein with all essential amino acids. With a fluffy texture and mild flavor, it serves as a perfect foil to a salad resplendent with the bounty of the summer's garden. The herb burnet adds the flavor of cucumbers.

In a saucepan, bring water or broth to a boil over medium-high heat. Stir in quinoa, cover, and reduce heat. Simmer for 10 to 15 minutes, or until tender. Remove from heat and cool for 30 minutes.

Combine all ingredients in a bowl and toss. Cover and refrigerate for at least 2 hours to allow the flavors to blend.
Yield: 8 servings

CHICKEN SALAD WITH DAYLILIES

❖

2 tablespoons lemon juice
¼ cup low-fat or reduced-calorie
   mayonnaise
2 tablespoons honey
1 teaspoon minced fresh tarragon
   leaves
8 sliced fresh daylily buds
½ teaspoon salt
¼ teaspoon ground black pepper
1¾ cups diced cooked chicken
¼ cup finely chopped fresh lovage
   stems and leaves
¼ cup chutney
1 tablespoon capers
1 tablespoon minced crystallized
   gingerroot
   Bibb lettuce leaves
4 open daylilies, with stamens
   and pistils removed

Edible flowers add color and flavor to all salads, but daylilies, with their "beany" essence, are particularly good. The best-flavored ones are the yellows and other pale colors. This recipe is adapted from Herbs & Imagination: "A Cure for Salad Boredom" *by Jean S. Fisher of The Herb Society of America — Wisconsin Unit.*

In a small bowl, combine lemon juice, mayonnaise, honey, tarragon, daylily buds, salt, and pepper. In a large bowl, combine chicken, lovage, chutney, capers, and ginger. Toss with the dressing. Chill.

For each individual serving, place some lettuce leaves on a plate. Place a daylily bloom on its side and add a serving of chicken salad spilling out of it, like a cornucopia.

Variation: Chop the chicken finely and use the salad as a filling for tea sandwiches. Decorate the serving platter with daylily blossoms.
Yield: 4 servings

Tomato and Tarragon Soup (page 34) ▶

Soups

TOMATO AND TARRAGON SOUP

Tarragon

The anise-licorice flavor of France's haute herb, tarragon, is repeated in the French liqueur Pernod. Tarragon's scientific species name (dracunculus) *and its common names in many languages mean "serpent" or "dragon," a reference to the coiling roots. To charm the beast in the kitchen, use tarragon with eggs, salads, cheese dishes, marinades, and sauces.*

> 2 tablespoons canola oil
> 2 cups chopped yellow onions
> 2⅔ pounds tomatoes, peeled,
>   seeded, and chopped
> ¼ cup chopped garlic
> ⅓ cup Pernod
> 1 bay leaf
> 1 cup water
> 2 slices white bread, toasted, crusts removed, and cut into
>   ½-inch cubes
> 2 tablespoons fresh tarragon leaves
> 1 tablespoon lemon juice
> 1 teaspoon salt
> ½ teaspoon ground black pepper

Heat the oil in a large saucepan over medium-high heat. Add the onions and cook, stirring, about 8 minutes, or until soft. Add the tomato, garlic, Pernod, and bay leaf and cook about 10 minutes, or until the tomatoes have broken down. Add the water and bread, reduce the heat to low, and simmer for 15 minutes. Remove from the stove and stir in the tarragon leaves, lemon juice, salt, and black pepper. Remove the bay leaf. In two batches, pour the mixture into a blender and purée. Serve immediately or refrigerate and serve cold.

Yield: 8 servings

THAI COCONUT SOUP WITH SHRIMP AND HERBS

The exotic redolence of ginger, lemongrass, chile peppers, and cilantro beguiles the palate in this savory soup rich with coconut milk. Canned coconut milk (not sweetened cream of coconut), lime leaves, and rice noodles are available at specialty food stores and Asian groceries.

Combine the lime juice, sesame oil, and garlic in a small bowl and set aside. Cut the top 2½ inches from the asparagus, saving the bottoms for stock or cream of asparagus soup. Heat the peanut oil in a large saucepan over medium-high heat. Add the shrimp and cook for about 30 seconds, until they just begin to turn color. Add the asparagus tops and cook another 30 seconds. Lower the heat to medium. Add the gingerroot, lemongrass, chile pepper, and lime leaves. Cook for 1 minute. Add the stock or broth and coconut milk and bring to a simmer. Do not let the mixture boil. Add the rice noodles and cook about 3 minutes, or until the asparagus is tender. Remove from the heat and stir in the reserved lime juice mixture. Let stand for 10 minutes to allow flavors to blend. Remove lime leaves and serve immediately, garnished with the cilantro.

Yield: 4 to 6 servings

2½ tablespoons lime juice
½ teaspoon light sesame oil
2 garlic cloves, minced
¾ pound asparagus spears, each about ⅜- to ½-inch in diameter
2 tablespoons peanut oil
½ pound medium shrimp, peeled and deveined
2 teaspoons minced fresh gingerroot
One 3-inch stalk fresh lemongrass, minced
2 teaspoons minced fresh red or green chile pepper, such as jalapeño, Thai, or serrano
3 lime leaves
1 cup vegetable stock or canned vegetable broth
Two 14-ounce cans unsweetened coconut milk, regular or low-fat
2 ounces rice noodles, broken in half (about 1 cup)
½ cup minced fresh cilantro leaves

BLACK BEAN SOUP

❖

Black bean soup is most often associated with Spanish-speaking New World countries. Including cumin and chili powder in this version gives a nod in that direction, even though the thyme and savory speak of the Old World. The combination has a comforting, old-fashioned appeal that draws you in like a cheering fire. And the large amount of garlic used should take care of any colds or vampires!

Thyme is among the most indispensable of culinary herbs, and its cascading growth makes it an ideal plant to soften the edges of containers.

1 pound dried black beans, soaked overnight in cold water and drained, or three 15- or 16-ounce cans of cooked black beans, rinsed and drained
3 tablespoons canola oil
3 cups chopped yellow onions
12 to 18 garlic cloves, peeled and crushed
Ten 4-inch sprigs fresh thyme
Five 4-inch sprigs fresh savory
1 bay leaf
2 tablespoons commercial chili powder
2 tablespoons ground cumin seeds
¾ teaspoon hickory-smoked salt
½ teaspoon ground cayenne pepper
One 16-ounce can crushed tomatoes
3 to 4 cups vegetable stock or canned vegetable broth
½ cup red wine vinegar
8 ounces low-fat or nonfat sour cream

In a large saucepan, heat the oil over medium-high heat. Add the onions and cook, stirring, about 10 minutes, or until soft. Do not let the onions brown. Add garlic, thyme, savory, bay leaf, chili powder, cumin, smoked salt, and cayenne. Stirring, cook about 3 minutes, or until thick and fragrant. Add the drained beans, tomatoes, and stock or broth. Bring to a simmer, reduce heat to low, and cook until beans are tender, or about 2 hours for dried beans. Add more liquid, if necessary. If using canned beans, cook for 30 minutes, cool, and refrigerate for at least 8 hours to allow flavors to blend; then reheat and continue as follows.

Just before serving, remove the thyme and savory stalks and the bay leaf. If desired, purée half the soup in a blender, food processor, or food mill, then return puréed mixture to the pan. Stir in the vinegar. Ladle into bowls and serve immediately with dollops of sour cream.
Yield: 6 to 8 servings

Oyster Chowder with Parsley and Thyme

❖

The name "chowder," which in New England connotes a thick milk-based soup or stew with shellfish and vegetables, most likely comes from the French word chaudière, or stew pot. Contention arises, however, over just which ingredients make a proper chowder. Arguments aside, this version relies heavily on tradition, with the chile pepper giving it a spicy tweak.

Put the bacon or salt pork in a lidded, medium-sized, heavy-bottomed saucepan and cook over medium-high heat to release the fat. Or, heat the oil. Add the onions and cook, stirring, for about 6 minutes, or until soft. Add the potatoes, drained oysters, thyme, and chile pepper. Cook, continuing to stir, for about 5 minutes, or until the potatoes lose their raw look. Pour in the milk, cream or evaporated milk, and reserved oyster liquid. Cover and cook for about 35 minutes, or until the potatoes are tender. Watch carefully so the mixture does not boil. Remove from the heat and stir in the parsley and black pepper. Serve immediately with croutons or crackers.

Yield: 4 to 6 servings

¼ pound hickory-smoked bacon or salt pork, finely chopped, or 2 tablespoons canola oil
2 cups chopped yellow onions
1 pound potatoes, peeled and cut into ½-inch pieces
2 dozen fresh small or medium oysters, drained and packing liquid reserved
1 tablespoon fresh thyme leaves
½ teaspoon minced fresh red or green chile pepper, such as jalapeño or serrano
3½ cups milk
½ cup heavy cream or evaporated skim milk
¼ cup chopped fresh parsley
½ teaspoon ground black pepper

Herb-Cheese Crackers

These rich morsels make a bowl of soup seem extra special. Experiment with different cheeses, herbs, and nuts, too!

In a large bowl, combine the flour, cheese, and thyme. Add the butter and cut in with a pastry blender until the mixture resembles coarse crumbs. Stir in the pine nuts.

In a small bowl, mix together the wine and egg. Pour the egg mixture over the flour mixture and mix just until blended. With your hands, shape the dough into a ball.

Cut the dough into two equal pieces. Shape each piece into an 8-inch log. Wrap each log in plastic wrap and refrigerate at least 4 hours.

Preheat oven to 400°F. Lightly coat two baking sheets with nonstick cooking spray or line with parchment. Cut each log into ¼-inch-thick slices and place 1 inch apart on the baking sheets. Bake for 10 to 12 minutes, or until golden. Transfer to wire racks to cool. Store in an airtight container in the refrigerator.

Yield: 48 crackers

1¼ cups unbleached or all-purpose flour
4 ounces freshly grated Romano or Parmesan cheese
1 tablespoon fresh thyme leaves
½ cup (1 stick) butter, cut into ½-inch pieces
¾ cup pine nuts, lightly toasted
2 tablespoons dry white wine or sherry
1 large egg, or ¼ cup egg substitute

SORREL VICHYSSOISE

This is every cook's opinion,
No savoury dish without
an onion.
But lest your kissing
should be spoiled,
Your onions must be fully
boiled.

— Dean Swift

Of palaces and peasants, sorrel's close relation to and ability to grow like a weed has yielded a plant with a strongly dual nature. Readily available as a springtime tonic to cottage gardeners, sorrel has also transcended to the world of haute cuisine. In this particular variation on a much-beloved theme, the delightful sourness of sorrel elegantly combines with the sweet pungency of leeks.

2 tablespoons butter
2 tablespoons canola oil
2 cups chopped yellow onions
3 medium leeks, or a quantity sufficient to yield 4 cups when the cleaned
     white portions are cut into 1-inch sections
1 pound potatoes, peeled and cut into ½-inch pieces
1 bay leaf
4 cups vegetable stock or canned vegetable broth
½ teaspoon ground mace or nutmeg
½ cup heavy cream or evaporated skim milk
½ cup milk
1 cup fresh sorrel leaves, stems and any thick midribs removed
½ teaspoon ground white pepper

Heat the butter and oil in a saucepan over medium heat. Add the onions and leeks and cook, stirring frequently, for about 8 minutes, or until soft. Add the potatoes and bay leaf and cook for another 3 minutes, continuing to stir. Add the stock or broth, bring to a simmer, reduce the heat to low, cover, and cook until potatoes are very tender, or about 20 minutes.

Remove the bay leaf. Stir in the mace or nutmeg, cream or evaporated milk, milk, and sorrel and cook just until hot. Remove from the heat and purée in a blender or food processor, doing it in two batches if necessary. Stir in the white pepper. Serve immediately or refrigerate and serve cold. Garnish with chive flowers and leaves.
Yield: 6 servings

Sorrel

NATIVE TO EUROPE, parts of Asia, North America, and Greenland, garden sorrel *(Rumex acetosa)* has been used for centuries as both a culinary and medicinal herb. The ancient Egyptians and Romans ate sorrel to counteract the effects of overindulgence from eating rich food. In medieval times, sorrel was grown as a common potherb and used in sauces for red meats. Laplanders used sorrel to curdle milk. Sorrel leaves are high in vitamin C, and they were at one time used to prevent scurvy.

Harvest sorrel leaves while young and tender, as they grow bitter and tough with age.

French, or Buckler, sorrel *(Rumex scutatus)* is more highly prized by chefs than garden sorrel. The flavor is milder, with definite undertones of lemon. It is much preferred for sorrel soup. Try adding a few leaves in combination with lettuce on a sandwich for a new twist on an old standby.

VEGETABLE-FISH CHOWDER

❖

1 tablespoon canola oil
1 cup chopped yellow onions
4 cups vegetable stock or canned
    vegetable broth
1 cup dry white wine
1 bay leaf
1 pound small red potatoes,
    quartered
1 pound peeled, seeded, and
    diced tomatoes, or one
    16-ounce can crushed tomatoes
½ pound green or yellow summer
    squash, diced
¼ pound fresh green beans,
    ends removed and cut into
    1-inch pieces
½ cup diced red bell pepper
2 tablespoons fresh marjoram,
    minced
1 pound skinless, boneless, firm
    white-fleshed fish, such as
    grouper, monkfish, or snapper
1 teaspoon salt
¼ teaspoon ground black pepper

For those who prefer or find equally appealing a tomato chowder, this is a quick and simply made version with the fragrance and flavor of marjoram.

In a large pot, heat oil over medium heat. Stir in the onions and cook for about 5 minutes, or until soft. Add stock or broth, wine, and bay leaf. Bring to a boil and add potatoes and tomatoes. Reduce heat to low, cover, and simmer for about 20 minutes, or until potatoes are tender.

Remove half the potatoes and 1 cup of the cooking liquid and purée in a blender or food processor. Return to the pan, stirring well. Raise heat to medium and add squash, beans, bell pepper, and 1 tablespoon of the marjoram. Cover and cook for 5 minutes. Stir in fish, cover, and cook about 5 minutes more, or until fish flakes easily. Stir in salt and pepper and cook just until heated through. Serve immediately, garnished with the remaining marjoram.

Yield: 8 servings

Grow a variety of basils to get a range of leaf colors and sizes as well as flavors, including lemon, cinamon, and anise.

LOVAGE-AND-BASIL SOUP

❖

The undertone of celery, contributed by the lovage, enhances this quick, easily made soup with a lovely pale green color. Increase the tanginess by using lemon basil. Or, augment the sweet-spicy aroma by mixing in some cinnamon basil. If your basil is in flower, garnish the soup with some of the blossoms.

2 tablespoons butter
1 tablespoon canola oil
2 cups chopped yellow onions
½ pound potatoes, peeled and cut into ½-inch pieces
¼ cup coarsely chopped fresh lovage stems and leaves
2 cups vegetable stock or canned vegetable broth
½ cup dry white wine
½ cup water
1 cup fresh basil leaves

Heat the butter and oil in a saucepan over medium-high heat. Add the onions and cook, stirring, for about 6 minutes, or until soft. Add the potatoes and lovage and cook, continuing to stir, for about 5 minutes, or until the potatoes lose their raw look and the lovage becomes soft. Add the stock or broth, wine, and water, and cover. Reduce heat to low and simmer until the potatoes are very tender, or about 30 minutes. Add the basil and cook for 30 seconds. Remove from heat and purée in a blender, food processor, or food mill. Serve immediately or refrigerate and serve cold.
Yield: 4 to 6 servings

VEGETABLE STOCK

Fresh homemade stock provides a background of flavor to soups and other dishes that cannot be duplicated. Although some consider vegetable stock to be less rich in flavor than meat-based stocks, this version stands up well in comparison.

8 cups water
1 cup dry white wine
1 yellow onion, chopped
2 garlic cloves, crushed
2 tomatoes, chopped
1 carrot, peeled and cut into ½-inch slices
1 leek, white and pale green part, cut into ½-inch slices
½ cup chopped fresh lovage or celery stems and leaves
4 ounces mushrooms, halved
Four 4-inch sprigs fresh thyme
Four 4-inch sprigs fresh parsley
2 bay leaves
1 teaspoon whole black peppercorns

In a large saucepan, combine all ingredients and bring to a boil over medium-high heat. Reduce heat and simmer for about 1 hour, or until a good, rich flavor develops. Strain, discarding solids, and cool before storing. Store in an airtight container in the refrigerator for up to 1 week. Alternatively, freeze in 2-cup or 4-cup containers for up to 1 month.
Yield: 8 cups

COLD BLUEBERRY SOUP

❖

2 cups blueberries
⅓ cup honey
1 teaspoon minced orange zest
1 tablespoon chopped orange
    mint or spearmint
2 teaspoons fresh or dried
    lavender flowers
1 tablespoon lemon juice or
    blueberry vinegar
1 cup buttermilk
1 cup half-and-half cream or
    evaporated skim milk
Fresh lavender flowers
Fresh mint leaves

Simultaneously tart and sweet, cold fruit soups are a Scandinavian specialty. Mint leaves and lavender flowers echo these taste sensations, which, when combined with blueberries, yield a rejuvenating indulgence for languid summer days. Serve this as a first course or dessert.

In a saucepan, combine the blueberries, honey, orange zest, mint, lavender, and lemon juice or vinegar. Cook over medium heat until boiling, then reduce heat to low and simmer, covered, for 20 minutes.

Remove from heat and purée in a blender, food processor, or food mill. Pour into a bowl with the buttermilk and half-and-half or evaporated milk and stir thorougly. Cover and chill for at least 4 hours. Garnish with fresh lavender flowers and mint leaves.

Variation: Substitute pitted fresh sweet cherries for the blueberries. *Yield: 4 to 6 servings*

Awake, O north wind; and come, thou south; blow upon my garden, that the spices thereof may flow out. Let my beloved come into his garden, and eat his pleasant fruits.

— The Song of Solomon 4:16

CREAMED GREEN BEAN SOUP
WITH SAVORY

.... ❖ ....

No collection of herb recipes would be complete without some combination of savory and beans, being as they are inviolate partners. Although the annual summer savory has a more delicate flavor, if you use only the most tender growth of winter savory the taste won't be overwhelming.

⅓ **pound potatoes, peeled and cut into ½-inch pieces**
1 **cup chopped yellow onions**
1 **pound fresh green beans, trimmed and cut into 1-inch**
   pieces, or two 10-ounce packages frozen green beans
2½ **cups vegetable stock or canned vegetable broth**
½ **cup dry white wine**
2 **tablespoons fresh savory leaves**
¼ **teaspoon ground black pepper**
1 **cup half-and-half cream or evaporated skim milk**

In a saucepan, combine the potatoes, onions, beans, stock or broth, wine, 1 tablespoon of the savory, salt, and black pepper. Bring to a boil over medium heat, cover, reduce heat to low, and simmer for 30 minutes, or until vegetables are very tender. Purée in a blender, food processor, or food mill. Return to the saucepan, stir in cream or evaporated milk, and reheat on low. Serve immediately or refrigerate and serve chilled. Garnish with remaining savory leaves, minced, and grated Parmesan cheese, if desired.
Yield: 6 to 8 servings

Savory

SAVORY'S LATIN NAME, *Satureja*, means "satyr," which hints at its ancient use as a stimulant and aphrodisiac. Monks were prohibited from growing it, but savory was a favorite Italian garden herb nonetheless.

The perennial winter savory differs in various ways from the annual summer savory. In the summer, there is very little difference in flavor between the two. In the fall, the flavor of winter savory may be harsh, but you can use it if you cut the quantity in half. Summer savory is used fresh or dried, whereas winter savory is best used fresh or frozen because the dried leaves are tough.

Winter savory is used commercially as a seasoning in salami. Winter savory was prized by the Romans as a disinfectant herb and was strewn liberally on floors or burned on fires. In the garden, winter savory is good for creating knot designs.

CHILLED HERB SOUP

2 tablespoons unsalted butter
2 tablespoons canola oil
1 pound sweet onions (such as Vidalia or Walla Walla), chopped
¼ cup unbleached or all-purpose flour
4 cups vegetable stock or canned vegetable broth
1 cup dry white wine
2 cups fresh parsley leaves
1 cup fresh chives or garlic chives
¼ cup fresh burnet leaves
2 tablespoons fresh thyme or lemon thyme leaves
⅔ cup low-fat or nonfat sour cream
1 teaspoon salt
¼ teaspoon freshly ground black pepper
1 tablespoon herb vinegar or lemon juice
Low-fat or nonfat sour cream
Minced fresh herbs or edible flowers

Celebrate the garden overflowing with herbs by making this chilled soup that delights the senses with its scents and flavors. All the herbs used are among the easiest to grow and are staples of herbal cooking as well.

In a large saucepan, heat the butter and oil over medium heat and stir in onions. Cook for about 8 minutes, or until onions are soft, stirring occasionally. Sprinkle flour over the top and cook, stirring, for 3 minutes. Stir in stock or broth and wine and cook, stirring, for 2 minutes, or until slightly thickened. Remove from heat and stir in parsley, chives, burnet, and thyme. Cool to lukewarm.

In a blender, purée soup in batches until very smooth. Whisk in sour cream, salt, and pepper. Refrigerate in a covered container for at least 4 hours but not more than 24. Just before serving, stir in vinegar or lemon juice. Serve immediately, garnished with dollops of sour cream and minced fresh herbs or edible flowers.

Yield: 8 servings

SOUP GARNISHES

Garnishes for soup can be as simple or as elaborate as time and inclination allow. Minced herbs that match or complement the soup are always appropriate. Cutting the herbs into thin slivers, or julienne, adds another texture. Be sure to use the edible flowers of herbs, too. Certain garnishes lend themselves to different soups, so don't hesitate to experiment.

For example, with thick soups, try herb croutons or grated cheese mixed with minced fresh herbs. For cream soups, consider chopped, toasted nuts with minced fresh herbs or a dollop of sour cream or yogurt mixed with minced fresh herbs.

LENTIL-SAGE SOUP

❖

A colorful soup rich in nutrients, this makes a satisfying meal with a salad and bread. Fresh sage is much more versatile in foods and certainly needs to be more widely used.

In a large saucepan, heat oil over medium heat. Add the onions and cook, stirring occasionally, for 3 to 5 minutes, or until soft. Add garlic and cook for 30 seconds. Add lentils, carrots, tomatoes, sage, bay leaf, and stock or broth. Bring to a simmer, stirring occasionally. Cover and reduce heat to low. Cook 25 to 30 minutes, or until lentils and carrots are tender.

Discard the bay leaf. Remove half of the soup and purée in a blender. Return to the rest of the soup and heat through. Stir in the lemon or lime juice, salt, and pepper. Serve immediately, garnished with shallots.

Yield: 4 servings

CRISPY FRIED SHALLOTS

Shallots are easily grown if they are planted in early fall and harvested the following year. Fried shallots are a Malaysian specialty, with the round red type being prevalent.

8 shallots
¼ cup canola oil

Soak the whole, unpeeled shallots in salt water for 5 minutes. Drain, peel, and slice thinly. Dry thoroughly on a cloth.

In a wok or small skillet, heat the canola oil over medium heat. Add the shallots and cook, stirring, until golden. Remove with a slotted spoon and drain on a cloth. These can be made ahead and stored in an airtight container.

2 tablespoons canola oil
1½ cups chopped yellow onions
1 garlic clove, minced
1 cup red lentils
1 cup finely chopped carrots
½ cup peeled, seeded, and chopped tomatoes
¼ cup minced fresh sage leaves
1 bay leaf
4 cups vegetable stock or canned vegetable broth
2 tablespoons fresh lemon or lime juice
1 teaspoon salt
¼ teaspoon ground black pepper
Crispy Fried Shallots (see recipe)

A chaise lounge nestled among container plantings allow you to relax surrounded by the scents of herbs in all their glory.

BETA SOUP WITH LOVAGE

Bouquet Garni

USED TO FLAVOR SOUPS, stews, and broth, a bouquet garni is a group of herbs either tied together with kitchen twine or placed in a cheese-cloth bag. The classic combination is bay leaf, thyme, and parsley. The herbs are removed before serving. For this soup, make a bouquet garni with 1 bay leaf, 2 sprigs fresh thyme, 2 sprigs fresh oregano, and 4 sprigs fresh parsley.

Information about beta-carotene and antioxidants fills the news. You won't have to bother taking dietary supplements on the day you make this nutrient-rich soup that is a meal in itself.

    1 tablespoon canola or olive oil
    1 cup diced yellow onions
    ¼ cup thinly sliced lovage stems
    2 garlic cloves, minced
 1½ cups thinly sliced carrots
    1 cup peeled and diced sweet potatoes
    1 cup peeled and diced winter squash
    1 cup peeled, seeded, and chopped tomatoes
    4 cups vegetable stock or canned vegetable broth
    ½ cup dry white wine
      Bouquet Garni (see box)
    ½ pound green beans, cut into 1-inch lengths, or one 10-ounce package frozen green beans, thawed
    ½ pound fresh kale, spinach, or Swiss chard, washed and chopped
    1 cup spinach rotelle or elbow pasta

In a large saucepan, heat the oil over medium heat. Add the onions and cook, stirring occasionally, for 3 to 5 minutes, or until soft. Add lovage and garlic and cook for 30 seconds. Add carrots, sweet potatoes, squash, tomatoes, stock or broth, wine, and bouquet garni. Bring to a simmer, stirring occasionally. Reduce heat to low, cover, and cook for 30 minutes, or until vegetables are tender. Add beans, greens, and pasta. Raise heat to medium and cook for 15 minutes, or until pasta is done. Remove bouquet garni and serve immediately. *Yield: 6 servings*

Fettucine with Mushrooms, Arugula, Parsley, and Thyme (page 48) ▶

Pasta & Vegetarian Main Courses

FETTUCINE WITH MUSHROOMS, ARUGULA, PARSLEY, AND THYME

❖

Drawing largely upon foods common to Italian country kitchens, this luxurious pasta dish tantalizes the palate with the peppery tang of arugula. A Mediterranean native, arugula is high in iron; both it and the parsley are rich with vitamins A and C.

1½ cups half-and-half cream or
    evaporated skim milk
1½ cups dry Marsala or Madeira
  2 tablespoons olive oil
  2 tablespoons butter
  1 pound assorted mushrooms,
    such as portobello, crimini,
    shiitake, or oyster, cut into
    ¼-inch-thick slices
 10 garlic cloves, finely chopped
 ½ cup finely chopped shallots
 ¼ cup fresh thyme leaves
1½ pounds dry fettucine pasta
  4 cups arugula, washed, dried,
    and stems removed
 ½ cup chopped parsley leaves
  1 teaspoon salt
 ½ teaspoon ground black pepper
 ½ cup grated Parmesan cheese

In a saucepan, combine the cream or evaporated skim milk and Marsala or Madeira and cook over medium heat until reduced by half.

In a large skillet, heat the oil and butter over medium-high heat until the butter foams, then subsides. Add the mushrooms and cook, stirring, for about 6 minutes, or until they give up their liquid. Add the garlic and shallots. Cook for about 1 minute, or until the garlic becomes aromatic. Add the thyme and cook for 2 minutes.

In a large pot of boiling salted water, cook the pasta for about 10 minutes, until tender but firm. When the pasta is 2 minutes from being done, turn up the heat to high under the mushroom mix and stir in the reduced cream mixture. Remove from heat. Drain the pasta, then return it to the pot. Add the mushroom mix, arugula, parsley, salt, and pepper. Cook over low heat, stirring, until the arugula is wilted but still green. Serve immediately, topped with grated Parmesan cheese.

Yield: 6 to 8 servings

If parsley were as scarce as sturgeon eggs and as rare as truffles, it would conceivably be one of the world's most sought-after herbs.

— Craig Claiborne

Parsley's luxuriant growth and bright green color enhance any planting, and the herb supplies a flavor- and nutrient-rich addition to almost any dish.

ROTELLE WITH EGGPLANT, TOMATO, PURPLE BASIL, AND OREGANO

Transport yourself to the Mediterranean with the fragrances and flavors that are so beloved there. Meaty eggplant and delectable, sun-ripened tomatoes paired with pungent oregano and spicy purple basil distill the essence of summer in this simple, quickly prepared sauce served over little wheels of pasta.

 2 eggplants (about 2 pounds), cut into ½-inch-thick slices
 2 tablespoons kosher, or coarse, salt
 3 pounds tomatoes, peeled, seeded, and chopped
10 garlic cloves, thinly sliced
⅓ cup fresh oregano leaves
3½ tablespoons balsamic vinegar
 1 tablespoon red wine vinegar
⅓ cup plus 3 tablespoons olive oil
 1 teaspoon salt
½ teaspoon ground black pepper
 1 cup fresh purple basil leaves, cut into thin strips
 1 pound dry rotelle pasta
½ cup grated Parmesan cheese

Put the eggplant slices in a colander and toss with the kosher salt. Set in the sink or over a bowl to drain for 1 hour. Rinse the eggplant and dry with a towel.

Combine the tomatoes, garlic, oregano, and balsamic and red wine vinegars in a large bowl and set aside.

Combine the eggplant slices with ⅓ cup olive oil in a large bowl. Prepare a gas or charcoal grill, or preheat the oven broiler. Shake excess oil from the eggplant and grill for about 5 minutes, or until golden. Turn and cook the other side for about 5 minutes, or until golden and soft. Let the eggplant cool, then cut each slice into six pieces and set aside in the bowl.

Heat 3 tablespoons olive oil in a large skillet over medium-high heat. Add the tomato mixture. Stirring frequently, cook for 4 minutes. Stir in the salt, pepper, and purple basil and cook for about 30 seconds, or just until the basil wilts. Add the mixture to the grilled eggplant.

While the tomatoes are cooking, prepare the rotelle by cooking in boiling salted water for about 10 minutes, or until tender but firm. Drain and toss with the eggplant-tomato mixture. Sprinkle with grated Parmesan cheese and serve hot, or refrigerate and serve cold.
Yield: 6 to 8 servings

Oregano

OREGANO HAS BEEN used in cooking for over 2,000 years. Popularly associated with pizza and other Italian foods, oregano leaves have a spicy, bittersweet flavor and aroma that naturally blends with tomato-based dishes and sauces. It also combines well with egg and cheese dishes, breads, marinades, stews, roasted peppers, mushrooms, summer squash, and eggplant. Use the fresh flowers in salads, sandwiches, omelets, herb cheese, and garnishes.

Many gardeners and cooks are disappointed when home-grown oregano plants have little flavor. Oregano that is commonly sold varies greatly in taste. The best varieties to use for cooking are Greek oregano, *O. vulgare* var. *prismaticum (hirtum)* or varieties sometimes called Italian or dark oregano. Flavor may vary not only with different types of soil but also with the amount of light and water.

ASIAN COLD NOODLES WITH PEANUT SAUCE

❖

¼ cup creamy peanut butter
3 tablespoons canola oil
2 tablespoons light sesame oil
1 teaspoon hot chile oil
1 teaspoon honey
2 teaspoons soy sauce
3 tablespoons rice wine vinegar
10 ounces fresh Chinese-style wheat noodles
⅓ cup thinly sliced fresh Thai or anise basil leaves (purple, cinnamon, or lemon basil may be substituted)
⅓ cup chopped fresh cilantro leaves
⅓ cup chopped fresh chives
1 tablespoon grated fresh gingerroot
½ tablespoon minced garlic
1 teaspoon ground black pepper
¾ cup bean sprouts

For those with a penchant for Thai-style food with its amalgam of disparate flavors and textures, this pasta energizes the senses with the sweet-and-sour peanut sauce embellished with basil, cilantro, chives, and garlic.

In a small bowl combine the peanut butter, canola, sesame, and chile oils, and honey. Place the bowl over a saucepan of hot water and mix until warm and smooth.

In a large bowl combine the soy sauce and vinegar. Pouring in a thin stream, add the peanut mixture, whisking continuously until mixture is emulsified.

Cook the noodles in a large saucepan of boiling salted water for about 4 minutes, or until tender but firm. Drain and cool. Add the noodles, basil, cilantro, chives, ginger, garlic, black pepper, and bean sprouts to the peanut mixture, tossing well. Refrigerate and serve cold.

Yield: 4 servings

ZITI WITH BLACK OLIVE SAUCE

❖

Not for the timid, this assertive, quickly prepared sauce was inspired by ingredients from an Italian pantry. Use an intensely flavored Greek oregano and flat-leaved parsley to achieve the most glorious effect.

¼ cup olive oil
6 garlic cloves, peeled and crushed
½ pound black oil-cured olives, pitted and quartered
4 tablespoons small capers, drained
2 tablespoons fresh oregano leaves
One 2-ounce can anchovies, drained and mashed
1 jalapeño pepper, cored, seeded, and minced
1 pound dry ziti pasta
½ cup minced fresh flat-leaf parsley leaves
½ cup grated Parmesan cheese

In a saucepan, heat the olive oil over medium heat, add the garlic cloves, and cook until golden, or about 3 minutes. Do not let them brown or the flavor will be bitter. Remove the pan from the heat and mash the garlic with the back of a fork. Return to the heat and add the olives, capers, oregano, anchovies, and jalapeño pepper. Cook, stirring, on medium-low heat for 15 minutes.

Cook the ziti in a large saucepan of boiling salted water for 10 to 12 minutes, or until tender but still firm. Drain and put into a large serving bowl. Pour the sauce over the ziti, and sprinkle with the parsley and Parmesan cheese. Toss and serve immediately.

Yield: 6 servings

HERB PESTO

For a quick meal of pasta, nothing tops it like pesto, the Italian sauce essentially made of basil, garlic, cheese, olive oil, and pine nuts. Experiment with substituting parsley or other herbs for some of the basil, and pecans or walnuts for the pine nuts. Small amounts of other herbs also add a depth of flavor; consider chives, garlic chives, marjoram, oregano, mint, tarragon, or sage. Use as a sauce for steamed vegetables, grilled fish or chicken or as a topping for focaccia, toasted slices of crusty bread, or omelets.

2 cups fresh basil leaves
Pinch of salt
1 to 2 garlic cloves
½ cup grated Parmesan or Romano cheese
½ cup extra-virgin olive oil
¼ to ½ cup pine nuts

Using a food processor, preferably with a plastic blade, combine basil leaves, salt, and 1 or 2 peeled and crushed garlic cloves until a coarse paste is formed. Next, process in the grated Parmesan and/or Romano cheese. With the processor running, slowly add the extra-virgin olive oil in a thin stream. To finish, process in the pine nuts.

Use immediately or store in the refrigerator with a ½-inch coating of olive oil on top. To freeze pesto, prepare without the cheese and cover with ½ inch of olive oil; add the cheese after thawing.

For a lower-calorie version, substitute low-fat vegetable stock or broth for half of the oil. For even fewer calories, use nonfat Parmesan or eliminate the cheese altogether.

To use fresh parsley, substitute 1 cup of it for 1 cup of the basil.

Yield: About 2 cups

PASTA SHELLS AND MELON WITH PARSLEY AND MINT

Parsley

NATIVE FROM
EUROPE to
western Asia,
parsley has
been used since
ancient times. Both
the Greeks and Romans
utilized it medicinally. Associated
with the god Hercules, parsley was
said to bring stamina to men and
horses alike; parsley wreaths
adorned both winning athletes and
heroes' graves. The Romans used it
to disguise the scent of alcohol on
their breath (the high chlorophyll
content makes it a natural breath
freshener). Today, oil of parsley is
used commercially to scent cosmetics and perfumes.

There are two distinct types of
parsley: the curly-leaf form,
Petroselinum crispum var. *crispum*,
and the flat-leaf, or Italian, form, *P.
crispum* var. *neopolitanum*. There are
a number of varieties of curly parsley, including 'Forest Green', which
keeps its color well in the cold, and
'Krausa', which has exceptional flavor. Flat-leaf parsley has a stronger
flavor than the curly. The sweetest
is 'Gigante d'Italia', also known as
Giant Italian.

Anyone who enjoys cooking most likely also enjoys reading cookbooks. The
Antipasto Table *by Michele Scicolone continually provides mouth-watering
ideas. This is one of her more intriguing recipes.*

  8 ounces dry small-shell pasta
  2 tablespoons extra-virgin olive oil
1½ cups finely chopped cantaloupe
  2 ounces prosciutto, finely chopped (about ½ cup)
  ¼ cup finely chopped fresh flat-leaf parsley leaves
  ¼ cup finely chopped fresh mint leaves
  2 tablespoons lemon juice
    Salt and freshly ground black pepper to taste

Bring a large pot of salted water to a boil over high heat. Add the
pasta. Cook, stirring occasionally, until the pasta is tender yet
still firm to the bite. Drain and toss the pasta in a large bowl
with the olive oil. Let cool completely.

Just before serving, add the cantaloupe, prosciutto, parsley, and
mint to the pasta. In a small bowl, combine the lemon juice with salt
and pepper to taste. Pour over the pasta and toss well.
Yield: 4 servings

Stir-Fried Tofu with Chinese Cabbage and Carrots

Fast-food that's healthy is the hallmark of this stir-fry with enticing flavors and scents. Garlic chives are easily grown and amazingly versatile. And not only in the kitchen: the flowers are charming in both fresh and dried arrangements.

To make the sauce, whisk together the cashew butter and hot water in a small bowl. Stir in the vinegar, soy sauce, honey, and hot red pepper sauce. Set aside.

To make the stir-fry, heat a wok or large nonstick skillet with the oil over medium-high heat. Add the onions, carrots, and ginger. Stir-fry the ingredients for 3 minutes. Add the tofu, Chinese cabbage, and cashews and stir-fry until the vegetables are tender-crisp, or 3 to 4 minutes. Stir in the sauce, scallions, and garlic chives. Cook about 1 minute, or until all the ingredients are hot. Serve immediately with cooked rice.

Yield: 6 servings

STIR-FRYING TIPS

Stir-frying involves cooking small pieces of food over relatively high heat while stirring continuously to prevent sticking. Although a wok is ideal, any large nonstick skillet is perfectly fine. Canola, safflower, and peanut oils readily withstand the high heat without burning. Before starting, have all ingredients cut up and measured, then arranged in the order that they'll be used. To save even more time, prepare ingredients ahead of time and refrigerate until ready to cook.

SAUCE

- ⅓ cup cashew butter
- ¼ cup hot water
- ¼ cup rice vinegar
- 2 tablespoons soy sauce
- 2 tablespoons honey
- ½ teaspoon hot red pepper sauce

STIR-FRY

- 1 tablespoon canola oil
- ½ cup chopped yellow onions
- ¼ pound carrots, thinly sliced on the diagonal
- 1 teaspoon minced fresh gingerroot
- 1 pound extra-firm tofu, drained and cut into ½-inch cubes
- ¼ pound Chinese cabbage, thinly sliced
- ½ cup dry-roasted, unsalted cashews
- ¼ cup chopped scallions
- 2 tablespoons chopped garlic chives

I want death to find me planting my cabbages.

— Michel Eyquen de Montaigne, *Essays*

LEEK QUICHE WITH THYME AND LAVENDER

❖

One 9-inch pie shell, unbaked, store-bought or homemade
1¼ cups grated Gruyere, Emmenthaler, or low-fat Swiss cheese
2 tablespoons butter
1 tablespoon canola oil
2 medium leeks, or a quantity sufficient to yield 2½ cups when the cleaned white portions are cut into ½-inch sections
2 tablespoons fresh thyme leaves
½ cup dry white wine
2 large eggs, lightly beaten, or ½ cup egg substitute
1 cup heavy cream or evaporated skim milk
1 tablespoon lavender flowers
½ teaspoon salt
½ teaspoon ground black pepper
⅛ teaspoon grated nutmeg
⅛ teaspoon ground cayenne

More commonly considered an essential ingredient in potpourri, lavender's bittersweet flavor most assuredly enhances food as well, be it salads, egg dishes, soups, or desserts.

Heat oven to 350°F. Line the pastry shell with parchment paper and put in ½-inch or so of pie weights or dried beans. Bake for 15 minutes; remove weights and parchment, reduce heat to 325°F, and bake for about 8 minutes more, or until the bottom is dry. Sprinkle ¼ cup grated cheese over the bottom of the crust and bake for about 5 minutes, or until the cheese is melted. Remove and cool.

In a large skillet, heat the butter and oil over medium-high heat until foaming subsides. Add the leeks and cook, stirring, for about 5 minutes, or until the leeks are soft. Stir in the thyme and cook for about 2 minutes, or until it is fragrant. Stir in the wine, reduce heat to medium, and cook, stirring, for about 3 minutes, or until all liquid is gone. Set aside and cool to room temperature.

In a large bowl combine the eggs or egg substitute, cream or evaporated milk, lavender, 1 cup grated cheese, salt, black pepper, nutmeg, and cayenne. Stir in the cooled leek mixture. Pour into the crust and bake at 350°F for about 35 minutes, or until the top is just set. Serve warm or cold.
Yield: 6 servings

BASIC SINGLE-CRUST

1½ cups unbleached flour
½ teaspoon salt
½ cup solid vegetable shortening
3 to 4 tablespoons water

Combine the flour and salt in a mixing bowl. Add the solid vegetable shortening. Working quickly with your fingertips, two knives, or a pastry blender, blend the ingredients until the mixture develops tiny, uneven flakes and bits the size of breadcrumbs. Sprinkle in the water, 1 tablespoon at a time, gently stirring with a fork after each addition. Add only enough water so the dough becomes a rough mass.

If desired, wrap dough in plastic wrap and refrigerate for up to 2 days. Or, roll it out immediately on a floured surface until it is ⅛-inch thick and about 12 inches in diameter, keeping the shape as round as possible. Fold in quarters and transfer to a 9-inch pie pan. Unfold and trim or pat edges to fit.
Yield: One 9-inch shell

Thyme

GROWN IN THE
ANCIENT GARDENS
of Babylon,
wonderfully
fragrant thyme was
initially used as a
strewing herb. No
surprise then that the
name *thymus* is derived from the
Greek *thuo*, "to perfume." A known
antiseptic, people carried it to
ward off the plague; Charlemagne
decreed that all herb gardens should
contain thyme.

Bees love the nectar of thyme
flowers and produce a favored
honey from them. In ancient
Greece, the thyme honey from
Mount Hymettus was world
famous. Lacking your own hive,
you can make flavored honey at
home by steeping thyme in store-
bought honey.

A digestive, thyme enhances
soups, chowders, and stuffings as
well as meat, fish, and cheese. The
herbal rule of thumb is, "When in
doubt, use thyme!" Essential to
bouquet garni, thymes are also useful
in barbecue, drinks, vinegars, mustard, and hot and cold drinks, especially tomato and carrot juices. The
first vegetable companions to consider with thymes are squash, eggplant, beans, and carrots; but you
should experiment with others.
Fruit- and spice-flavored thymes
work well with fruits and desserts.
The edible flowers serve as garnish
and flavoring, too.

Ripe Jalapeño, Potato, and Monterey Jack Omelet

.... ❖ ....

When ripe, the bright red jalapeño pepper develops a bit of sweetness to complement its hotness. Smokey-tasting fresh sage and the nuttiness of cumin round out the pleasure in this hearty omelet reminiscent of the Southwest. A fresh tomato salsa is the ideal accompaniment.

½ **pound new potatoes (each about 1½ inches in diameter), thinly sliced**
1 **tablespoon butter**
½ **cup ripe jalapeño pepper, cored, seeded, and minced**
6 **large eggs or 1½ cups egg substitute**
2 **tablespoons milk**
1 **tablespoon thinly sliced fresh sage leaves**
½ **teaspoon ground cumin seeds**
½ **teaspoon salt**
1 **tablespoon canola oil**
2 **ounces shredded low-fat Monterey Jack cheese (about ½ cup)**

If the sage bush thrives and grows, the master's not master, and he knows.

— Anonymous

Cook the potatoes in boiling salted water for about 20 minutes, or until tender. Drain.

Melt the butter in a small nonstick skillet over medium heat and cook the jalapeño pepper for about 3 minutes, until soft.

In a medium bowl, beat the eggs or egg substitute, milk, sage, cumin, and salt with a fork or whisk.

In a large nonstick skillet or omelet pan, heat the oil over high heat. Pour the egg mixture into the skillet. With a nonmetallic fork or whisk, keep the bottom of the omelet moving while tilting the pan and cook for about 30 seconds. Without stirring, cook for about 15 seconds more, or until the bottom is set. Remove from heat.

Sprinkle the cheese, jalapeño pepper, and potatoes over the top. Gently slide the omelet away from the pan handle while hitting the handle with your fist. This should curl the far side of the omelet. Hold the pan at a 45-degree angle away from the handle above a plate, with the pan just touching it. With a spatula, slip the near side of the omelet over the center and turn the handle over the plate, to fold the omelet in thirds. Cut in half and serve immediately.

Yield: 2 to 4 servings

COUSCOUS-THYME CRUST WITH VEGETABLE-PARSLEY FILLING

Couscous is semolina flour made into small granules that "cook" quickly when boiling liquid is poured over them. If you can't find the whole wheat form, use couscous made from bleached flour. Somewhat resembling a quiche, the couscous combined with fresh vegetables, beans, and parsley yields a nutritious meal high in fiber. This recipe uses only egg whites and low-fat cheese to reduce the fat content.

Heat oven to 350°F. Spray a 10-inch deep-dish pie pan with non-stick cooking spray. In a small saucepan, bring stock or broth to a boil over medium-high heat. Stir in couscous, cover, and remove from heat. Let stand 5 minutes. Lightly fluff with a fork. Stir in egg whites and thyme, mixing thoroughly. Pour the couscous mixture into the pie pan and, with the back of a spoon, press evenly over the bottom and sides.

In a large saucepan, combine tomatoes, squash, mushrooms, and onion. Cook over medium heat, stirring occasionally, 8 to 10 minutes, or until vegetables are tender. Remove from heat and stir in beans, parsley, and ¼ cup cheese, mixing well.

Spoon the vegetable mixture into the couscous-lined pie pan. Bake 25 to 30 minutes, or until crust and vegetables are beginning to turn golden. Sprinkle the remaining ¼ cup cheese over the top. Return to the oven for about 5 minutes, or until cheese is melted. Let sit for a few minutes, then cut into wedges and serve.

Yield: 6 servings

1 cup vegetable stock or canned vegetable broth
1 cup whole wheat couscous, uncooked
2 large egg whites
2 tablespoons minced, fresh thyme
2 cups peeled, seeded, and chopped tomatoes
2 cups thinly sliced green or yellow summer squash
1½ cups thinly sliced mushrooms
½ cup chopped yellow onions
One 15- or 16-ounce can pinto beans, rinsed and drained
¼ cup minced fresh parsley
½ cup shredded low-fat Monterey Jack cheese with hot peppers

VEGETABLE BURRITOS

.... ❖ ....

Eight 8-inch flour tortillas
2 tablespoons canola oil
½ cup finely chopped onion
¼ pound summer squash,
    finely chopped
Kernels from 1 ear of fresh corn
    or ½ cup frozen corn
½ pound fresh tomatillos (husks
    removed), washed and finely
    chopped
½ cup finely chopped sweet red
    pepper
½ cup finely chopped Anaheim
    chile pepper
1 jalapeño pepper, seeded and
    finely chopped
2 garlic cloves, finely chopped
⅓ cup shelled pumpkin seeds,
    toasted
2 tablespoons lime juice
1 tablespoon chopped fresh
    cilantro leaves
1 teaspoon chopped fresh
    oregano leaves
½ teaspoon ground cumin
1 cup nonfat sour cream
1 cup finely chopped avocado,
    tossed with 1 tablespoon
    lemon juice
Fresh Tomato Salsa (see recipe)

A light, nutritious meal brimming with the best of the summer garden, these burritos feature sautéed New World vegetables seasoned with piquant herbs and hot peppers.

Heat oven to 350°F. Wrap the tortillas in aluminum foil and heat in the oven about 10 minutes, or until warm and soft. Meanwhile, heat the oil in large skillet over medium-high heat. Add onion and cook, stirring, about 5 minutes, or until soft. Stir in zucchini, corn, tomatillos, sweet red pepper, Anaheim pepper, jalapeño pepper, garlic, pumpkin seeds, lime juice, cilantro, oregano, and cumin and cook about 5 minutes, or until all the vegetables are tender and crisp.

Spoon about ½ cup of the vegetable mixture onto the center of each warm tortilla. Fold one end of tortilla up about 1 inch over mixture; fold right and left sides over folded end, overlapping. Fold remaining end down. Place two tortillas, seam side down, on each plate. Serve immediately, garnished with a dollop of sour cream and sprinkled with the avocado and salsa.
Yield: 4 servings

FRESH TOMATO SALSA

⅔ pound tomatoes, peeled,
    seeded, and finely chopped
½ cup finely chopped sweet
    green pepper
¼ cup finely chopped onion
1 jalapeño pepper, cored, seeded,
    and finely chopped
1 garlic clove, finely chopped
2 teaspoons minced fresh
    cilantro leaves
1 teaspoon olive oil
½ teaspoon salt

Nothing can compare with salsa made from just-picked, sun-ripened tomatoes, peppers, and cilantro!

Prepare the salsa by combining all ingredients in a bowl. Use immediately, or cover and refrigerate for up to 3 days.
Yield: About 1½ cups

Garlic

CONSIDERED SINCE ANCIENT TIMES to have both magical and medicinal powers for warding off evil and strengthening the body, garlic abounds with legends, myths, and facts. In the *Iliad*, Odysseus cast a spell on Circe with garlic. Early Egyptians, Israelites, and Romans ate it for the stamina it provided. It also supposedly discourages vampires and unwanted beaus.

From earliest times, garlic has been prescribed as a medicine for a wide range of ailments, including high blood pressure, respiratory problems, sore throats, headaches, hysteria, worms, tumors, plagues, earaches, and depression. Some of these claims have been substantiated, as garlic inhibits bacteria, fungi, yeast, and parasites when in its fresh, crushed state. Garlic has also been shown to thin the blood and reduce cholesterol levels. Rich in vitamin A, it also contains vitamin C, B vitamins, magnesium, phosphorus, potassium, and protein.

The pungent richness of garlic forms the base for all other savory flavorings. When sautéeing in oil or butter, cook garlic briefly until just softened, being careful not to let it become brown and bitter. Roasted garlic deserves its vaunted status; get in the habit of making and using it!

PASTA, BEANS, AND GREENS

‖❖‖

12 ounces dry short whole wheat
   pasta such as rigatoni,
   mostaccioli, or farfelle
2 cups coarsely chopped fresh
   spinach, kale, Swiss chard, or
   other greens
   One 15- or 16-ounce can Great
   Northern, garbanzo, or pinto
   beans, rinsed and drained
1 cup vegetable broth or stock
½ cup minced fresh herbs
2 ounces crumbled feta, goat, or
   blue cheese

Although herbs are often interchangeable in recipes, this healthful combination of whole grain pasta, beans, and greens is particularly open to various adaptations. Mediterranean herbs such as thyme, rosemary, and marjoram are the traditional choices, but don't hesitate to try tarragon, any of the basils, nasturtium leaves and flowers, fennel, dill, or cilantro as well as any other of your favorites.

In a large pot of boiling salted water, cook the pasta for about 15 minutes, or until just tender. Stir in the greens and cook for another minute. Drain and return mixture to the pot. Stir in the beans, broth or stock, and herbs and cook until just heated through. Transfer to a serving platter and sprinkle with cheese. Serve immediately or at room temperature.
Yield: 6 servings

VEGETABLE PATTIES

‖❖‖

1 cup peeled and grated Yukon
   Gold potato
1 cup peeled and grated sweet
   potato
1 cup grated carrot
½ cup finely chopped onion
1 cup finely chopped fresh kale,
   Swiss chard, arugula, or spinach
½ cup whole wheat flour
1 tablespoon minced fresh sage
   leaves
1 tablespoon minced fresh thyme
   leaves
1 teaspoon minced fresh savory
   leaves
2 garlic cloves, minced
1 small fresh red or green chile
   pepper, seeded, and minced
1 large egg, lightly beaten, or
   ¼ cup egg substitute
1 teaspoon salt
¼ teaspoon ground black pepper
   Canola or olive oil or nonstick
   oil spray

Once rare, "veggie burgers" are now almost ubiquitous. Although most of the commercial ones are grain-based, this homemade version features instead fresh vegetables high in beta-carotene and other nutrients. The herbs chosen gild the lily with their rich, satisfying flavor.

Combine all ingredients in a large bowl. Form ¼ cup of the mixture into a 3-inch-diameter patty. Place on a large baking sheet. Repeat with remaining mixture. Refrigerate for 1 hour.
In a large nonstick skillet, heat a small amount of oil or oil spray over medium heat. Cook vegetable patties about 5 minutes per side, or until golden. If all the patties do not fit in the skillet, cook them in batches. Serve immediately.
Yield: 6 servings (12 patties)

FRIED GREEN TOMATO-AND-BASIL SANDWICHES

⬥

A down-home southern favorite goes upscale when paired with basil and then made into a satisfying sandwich. The technique for frying the tomatoes is adapted from Ronni Lundy, author of Shuck Beans, Stack Cakes, and Honest Fried Chicken.

- **4 green tomatoes (about 2 pounds)**
- **1 cup unbleached or all-purpose flour**
- **1 teaspoon salt**
- **⅛ teaspoon ground black pepper**
- **⅔ cup buttermilk**
- **Canola oil**
- **8 slices whole wheat bread, toasted**
- **2 tablespoons low-fat or reduced-calorie mayonnaise**
- **Enough basil leaves to cover 4 sandwiches**

Slice tomatoes ½ inch thick. In a flat bowl combine flour, salt, and pepper. Pour the buttermilk into another flat bowl. Pour oil in a heavy skillet to ⅛ inch deep. Heat the oil over high heat until a speck of flour dropped in dances around.

Dip the tomato slices in the buttermilk, then in the flour mixture, coating both sides. Lay each slice gently in the oil. Lower the heat to medium. Fry until golden brown on one side, then turn and fry until golden on the other side. Remove with a slotted spatula and drain on paper towels.

Toast the whole wheat bread. Spread the mayonnaise on four slices of toast, and then distribute the basil leaves. Top with tomato slices and the remaining slices of toast. Serve immediately.

Yield: 4 servings

Basil

NATIVE TO ASIA, Africa, and South and Central America, basils come in a great number of shapes, sizes, and flavors.

Common sweet basil *(Ocimum basilicum)* grows about 24 to 36 inches tall with 2- to 3-inch, smooth, bright green leaves. One of the best-flavored varieties of common basil is variously labeled as Perfume, Genoa, or Genovese. It has compact growth and dark, glossy green leaves. Lettuce leaf basil *(O. frutescens)* has foliage up to 6 inches long.

Dwarf, or bush, basil *(O. basilicum* 'Minimum') has tiny ½-inch leaves on plants 8 to 12 inches tall. The variety 'Spicy Globe' forms very rounded dwarf plants. There is also a dwarf variety with purple leaves *(O. basilicum* 'Purpurascens Minimum'), as well as two types of larger plants with purple leaves: purple basil *(O. basilicum* 'Purpurascens') and dark opal basil *(O. purpurem)*. These have purple flowers as well. The varieties 'Purple Ruffles' and 'Green Ruffles' have leaves that are very puckered. Sweet-fine basil *(O. compactus)* has small, fruit-scented leaves on 18-inch plants.

GRILLED EGGPLANT-CHEESE SANDWICHES WITH GARLIC, MINT, AND THYME

Eggplant has been cultivated in India for thousands of years. Blessed with an intriguing flavor and rich in antioxidants, it offers many culinary opportunities and blends well with a wide range of herbs. Given the opportunity, grow or purchase the long, skinny Asian eggplants, which have a sweet, nutty flavor — and provide the perfect sized slices for these sandwiches! 'Ichiban' and 'Tycoon' are two of the best Asian eggplant varieties.

- 1 pound Asian eggplants, cut horizontally in ¼-inch-thick slices
  Olive oil nonstick cooking spray
- 1 head roasted garlic (see page 15), removed from skins and mashed
- 2 tablespoons low-fat or reduced-calorie mayonnaise
- 1 teaspoon balsamic or sherry vinegar
- 1 whole wheat baguette, about 18 inches long
- ¼ cup fresh mint leaves
- 2 tablespoons fresh thyme or lemon thyme leaves
- 2 ounces fresh goat cheese, homemade yogurt cheese, or feta cheese, crumbled

Prepare grill or heat oven broiler. Spray both sides of eggplant slices with olive oil. Cook eggplant 3 to 5 minutes, or until tender and golden, turning once. Transfer eggplant to a platter.

In a small bowl whisk together the roasted garlic, mayonnaise, and vinegar.

Cut bread into 4 pieces and halve each piece horizontally. Spread bottom halves with the mayonnaise mixture. Sprinkle with the mint and thyme, then top with eggplant slices, cutting to fit, if necessary. Sprinkle on crumbled cheese. Cover with remaining pieces bread. Serve immediately.

Yield: 4 servings

Mint

RAPACIOUS MINTS, overtaking gardens around the world, are beloved nonetheless for their cool, refreshing tang. Mainly native to far-flung lands from Europe to Asia, mints have been valued since the time of the ancient Egyptians as tokens of esteem, barter, medicine, or flavoring. In herbal lore, mint is the symbol of hospitality.

Because mints spread rampantly from invasive roots, they are ideal for container growing, which will keep them in bounds yet still produce an abundant supply. Grow different varieties in separate containers.

Although there are only about 25 true species of mint, natural and artificial hybridization has yielded several thousand variations, with much confusion as to the correct naming of all of them.

The different varieties of spearmint are the best for cooking, whether with various meats, beans and grains, soups, vegetables, or desserts; or made into herb butters and vinegars. Peas, potatoes, carrots, cucumbers, and tomatoes are particularly good with mint.

(recipe on page 64) *Grilled Shrimp with Citrus and Herbs* ▶

Fish
Main Courses

GRILLED SHRIMP WITH CITRUS AND HERBS

❖

2 limes, thinly sliced
1 lemon, thinly sliced
3 tablespoons olive oil
2 tablespoons Galliano or
  anisette liqueur
1 tablespoon tequila
1 teaspoon dried hot red pepper
  flakes
4 garlic cloves, thinly sliced
Ten 4-inch sprigs of fresh herbs
2½ pounds large shrimp, in
  the shell

Nowhere is the dictum to be bold and daring with different herbs more applicable than with this simply prepared grilled shrimp. Experiment with the different thymes or basils as well as oregano, marjoram, fennel, or tarragon.

Combine all ingredients in a large bowl or dish, cover, and refrigerate for 4 to 6 hours, stirring occasionally. Prepare the grill. Remove the shrimp from the marinade, place on a metal skewer, and grill for about 2 minutes on each side. Both sides should be red and the center of the head end opaque.
Yield: 4 servings

BAKED BROOK TROUT STUFFED WITH SORREL

❖

4 whole boneless 10-ounce brook
  trout, head and skin on
2 cups small sorrel leaves, or
  large leaves torn in half
3 tablespoons olive oil
1 large yellow onion (about
  ⅓ pound) cut into thin strips
2 medium tomatoes (about
  ⅔ pound) peeled, seeded,
  and cut into small strips
½ cup dry white wine
½ teaspoon salt
¼ teaspoon ground black pepper

The lemony tang of sorrel is at its best with the new growth of spring. Don't ignore it the rest of the time, however. Just select the smallest, tenderest leaves.

Open the trout and lightly salt and pepper the inside. Spread ½ cup of sorrel in each cavity and fold the trout over. If you are unable to close the trout, redistribute the sorrel or take some out, but remember that it will cook down.

Preheat oven to 350°F. In an ovenproof skillet or pan large enough to hold the trout, heat the oil over medium-high heat. Add the onion and tomatoes and cook, stirring, for about 5 minutes, or until they soften. Add the wine and bring to a simmer. Lay the trout over the mixture and bake for 5 minutes. Using a long spatula, carefully turn the trout over without dislodging the sorrel, which should be half-cooked. Bake for another 5 minutes, or until the thickest part of the flesh is just opaque. Place the trout on serving plates. Add the salt and pepper to the pan, and spoon the cooking liquid over the fish.
Yield: 4 servings

STRIPED BASS WITH BRAISED LEEKS

◆

One of the great flavor combinations is rosemary and dry vermouth. Something in the camphorous quality of the rosemary and the herb-flavored wine fits well together. Often used with chicken, the combination here offsets the sweet richness of the fish and leeks.

Cook the bacon in a large, lidded, heavy-bottomed skillet over medium-high heat until just beginning to brown. Or, heat the olive oil. Add the leeks and rosemary and cook for 5 minutes, until the leeks begin to soften. Add the vermouth and stock or broth. Reduce the heat to low and cover. Cook for 7 to 8 minutes, until the leeks are tender.

Preheat oven to 350°F. Transfer the leeks and liquid to a lidded ovenproof dish just large enough for the fillets to fit side by side. Salt and pepper the fish and lay the fillets over the leeks, skin side up. Sprinkle the fillets with lemon juice, then brush on the melted butter. Cover and bake for 10 to 12 minutes, or until the fish flakes easily with a fork. Serve immediately.

Yield: 6 to 8 servings

2 ounces smoked bacon, diced, or 2 tablespoons olive oil
3 medium leeks, or a quantity sufficient to yield 4 cups when the cleaned white portions are cut into ¾-inch sections
2 tablespoons chopped fresh rosemary leaves
½ cup dry white vermouth
½ cup vegetable stock or canned vegetable broth
2 pounds striped bass fillets, skin on and boneless
2 tablespoons lemon juice
2 tablespoons butter, melted

BAKED FISH WITH OATMEAL-HERB CRUST

◆

Certainly food needn't be complicated to be good, as these herb-crusted fish fillets show. Serve them as a healthful main course with a low-fat fruit salsa or on homemade bread as a sandwich. This recipe is adapted from one by Helen Trueblood of The Herb Society of America — Kentuckiana Unit.

Place the fish fillets in an ovenproof dish large enough to hold them in a single layer. In a small bowl, whisk together oil, lemon juice, and 1 tablespoon minced herbs. Pour over the fish and let marinate for 30 minutes.

In a blender combine the oats, remaining 3 tablespoons of herbs, salt, and pepper. Heat oven to 450°F. Dip the fillets in the oatmeal mixture and place on a baking sheet or pan coated with nonstick cooking spray. Bake for 8 to 10 minutes, or until the fish flakes easily.

Yield: 4 to 6 servings

1½ pounds skinless, boneless fish fillets, such as whitefish or perch
2 tablespoons canola oil
2 tablespoons lemon juice
¼ cup minced fresh herbs, such as tarragon, chervil, fennel, parsley, thyme, basil, chives, garlic chives, or savory, alone or in combination
½ cup old-fashioned rolled oats
½ teaspoon salt
¼ teaspoon ground black pepper

STEAMED MUSSELS WITH FRENCH HERBS

***

Because the herbs are added at the last minute, they deliver bracing, zestful flavor at its peak. If chervil is unavailable, substitute tarragon. The onion-like yet distinctive flavor of shallots gives an important background to the other herbs. And don't worry about the quantity of garlic — it will mellow and blend with all the others.

Chervil is the noble cousin of the parsleys. The flavor of chervil is so tender that it should be used more generously than other herbs.

— Leonia De Sounin, *Magic in Herbs*

2 tablespoons butter
1 tablespoon canola oil
1 cup finely chopped shallots
¼ cup finely chopped garlic
¾ cup dry white wine
5 pounds mussels, scrubbed and debearded
⅓ cup extra-virgin olive oil
3 tablespoons lemon juice
½ cup chopped fresh chervil leaves
½ cup chopped fresh parsley leaves
½ cup chopped fresh thyme leaves
½ cup chopped fresh chives

Melt the butter with the oil in a large saucepan over medium-low heat. Add the shallots and garlic and cook for about 4 minutes, or until they begin to soften. To make sure they don't brown, stir them frequently and lower the heat if necessary. Add the wine. Bring to a boil and add the mussels. Cover and steam for 6 minutes.

Check to see that most of the mussels are open. If not, cook for another minute. Pour the mussels into a large colander over a bowl. Shake the colander to collect all the cooking liquid, and transfer it to a small saucepan. Over high heat, reduce the liquid by half.

Meanwhile, sort through the mussels and remove any that are stubbornly shut. Remove the top shell from the remaining mussels and distribute them between six shallow bowls.

Combine 1 cup of the reduced liquid, the olive oil, and the lemon juice in a blender, then return the emulsion to the saucepan. Stir in the herbs and cook just until the mixture is warmed. Pour over the mussels. Serve with loaves of French bread and a salad.
Yield: 6 servings

Chervil

CHERVIL IS NATIVE
to southeastern
Europe and has
attained its
greatest popularity
in French cuisine.
Growing best in the cool
temperatures of spring and
fall, chervil has a delicate, anise-like
flavor. It can be used in greater
quantity than most herbs.

Chervil is an excellent addition to
green salads or, when minced, to
vinaigrette dressing. Also use it
with vegetables, cream soups,
omelets, and cheese dishes.

Chervil's delicate flavor is lost
when cooked for longer than
10 minutes, so add it near the end
of cooking. Its flavor is also lost
when dried, so preserve it by using
it to flavor vinegar.

Fresh chervil leaves are essential
to the French *fines herbes*, a mixture
of chervil, chives, parsley, and
tarragon. Try this mélange in herb
butters, soups, sauces, egg dishes,
vegetables, and fish.

GRILLED SWORDFISH WITH RED ONION, MANGO, AND CHILE SALSA

1½ cups chopped mango
1½ cups chopped papaya
1 cup finely chopped red bell pepper
1 cup chopped fresh cilantro leaves
1½ cups finely chopped red onion
½ cup finely chopped fresh chile peppers
6 tablespoons lime juice
2½ tablespoons red wine vinegar
2 tablespoons lemon juice
2 tablespoons olive oil
2 teaspoons ground cumin seeds
1 teaspoon salt
1 teaspoon ground black pepper
4 swordfish steaks (each about 6 ounces)

This version of the popular Mexican–Latin American salsa is full of intense, conflicting flavors that are typical of the best. In addition to swordfish, this uncooked condiment is an excellent accompaniment to other grilled fish or steak, stews, steamed vegetables, rice, or beans. Use whatever combination of fresh chile peppers your palate prefers.

To make salsa, combine all ingredients except the fish in a large bowl, mixing well. Cover and let stand for 2 hours, allowing flavors to blend. Prepare a grill or heat the oven broiler. For 1-inch thick fish steaks, cook for 5 minutes. Turn and cook for 5 minutes on the other side. Serve topped with salsa.
Yield: 4 servings

GRILLED SALMON WITH BURNET-YOGURT SAUCE

This Middle East–inspired sauce has the flavor of cucumber subtly enhanced by the addition of burnet leaves. Ginger in the marinade contributes a spiciness; the mint brings sweetness; rosemary adds a resinous flavor. If you want to poach rather than grill the salmon and serve it chilled, omit the oil and cook in stock or dry white wine. To make salsa, the sauce would work just as splendidly.

Combine the oil, ginger, garlic, mint, and rosemary in a dish large enough to hold the salmon in a single layer. Add the salmon, turning to coat. Cover and let stand at room temperature for 1 hour.

Pour the yogurt in a strainer lined with a double layer of cheese-cloth. Let drain for an hour. This will make a thicker sauce without the usual tang of yogurt. Put the cucumber slices in another strainer or colander and sprinkle with the kosher salt. Toss and let drain in the sink for an hour. Rinse with cold water, drain, and pat dry with a towel. Purée the yogurt, cucumber, burnet, cumin, and lemon juice in a blender. Pour into a serving bowl, cover, and refrigerate.

Prepare a grill or heat the oven broiler. Remove the salmon from the marinade and wipe off excess oil. Salt and pepper the fillets and cook for about 5 minutes, until they can be turned easily. Don't try to turn fish that doesn't want to go — when the meat is caramelized, it will come up without a problem. Cook the fish on the other side for about 3 minutes more, until medium-rare. Serve hot with the burnet-yogurt sauce.

Yield: 6 servings

½ cup olive oil
One 1-inch piece fresh gingerroot, thinly sliced
3 garlic cloves, peeled and crushed
Four 4-inch sprigs fresh spearmint leaves
Two 4-inch sprigs fresh rosemary leaves
Six 6- to 8-ounce salmon steaks or skinless and boneless fillets
1½ cups plain nonfat yogurt
1 cup peeled, seeded, and thinly sliced cucumber
1 cup fresh burnet leaves
2 teaspoons ground cumin seeds
1½ teaspoons lemon juice
Salt and freshly ground black pepper to taste

Herbs get me more excited than anything else that grows, I think.

— Edna St. Vincent Millay

SQUID WITH THAI HERBS

$\diamondsuit$

¼ cup lime juice
2 teaspoons sugar
½ jalapeño pepper, cored, seeded, and minced
1 tablespoon minced lemongrass stalks
2 garlic cloves, minced
1 tablespoon fish sauce (nam pla)
1½ cups Chinese cabbage, cut into 1-inch slices
½ cup finely sliced scallions
½ cup fresh cilantro leaves
½ cup fresh mint leaves
¼ cup fresh basil leaves, torn into pieces if large
⅓ cup roasted, unsalted peanuts, chopped
2 tablespoons peanut or canola oil
2 pounds squid, cleaned and cut into ½-inch rings

Be adventurous! If you think basil is just for pesto, cilantro for salsa, and peppermint for chewing gum, you're in for a surprise. This is a Thai-style main course, generally eaten cold but just as good with the squid hot out of the pan. If you don't care for squid, this is also authentic with shrimp. Substitute ⅔ pound of medium shrimp, peeled and deveined.

To make the dressing, combine the lime juice, sugar, jalapeño pepper, lemongrass, garlic, and fish sauce in a small bowl. Set aside for at least 30 minutes.

Combine the cabbage, scallions, cilantro, mint, basil, and peanuts in a large bowl. Heat the oil in a large skillet over high heat. Add the squid and sauté for 45 seconds, until just opaque. Do not overcook, or it will toughen. Remove from the heat and add squid to the cabbage mixture. Pour on the dressing and toss. Cover and chill, or serve immediately. Accompany with cellophane noodles or rice.
Yield: 4 servings

ORANGE ROUGHY WITH TAHINI, TARRAGON, AND PARSLEY

$\diamondsuit$

2 pounds orange roughy fillets
3 tablespoons sesame or canola oil
¼ cup lemon juice
2 tablespoons minced fresh tarragon leaves
2 garlic cloves, minced
¾ pound sweet onion (such as Vidalia or Walla Walla), peeled and sliced
¼ cup tahini
⅓ cup vegetable stock or water
2 tablespoons minced fresh parsley leaves

Fish prepared with tahini, or ground sesame seeds, is traditional in Syria and Lebanon. In place of tarragon, try marjoram, oregano, or basil.

Place fish fillets in a shallow dish. Combine 1 tablespoon oil, 1 tablespoon lemon juice, 1 tablespoon tarragon, and half the garlic and pour over the fish. Cover and refrigerate for 1 hour.

Heat oven to 325°F. Warm the remaining 2 tablespoons of oil in a skillet over medium-high heat and stir in onions. Cook, stirring, for about 5 minutes, or until onions are soft and golden. Spread half the onions in a shallow, ovenproof dish and put fish on top in a single layer. Cover with remaining onions. Combine the tahini, 3 tablespoons lemon juice, 1 tablespoon tarragon, remaining garlic, and stock or water, stirring until smooth. Pour over the fish and bake for 30 minutes, or until the fish flakes easily. Serve immediately, sprinkled with fresh parsley.
Yield: 6 servings

CREPES WITH CURRIED SHRIMP AND MINT

❖

A most unusual combination but one definitely worth trying, particularly since this meal can be quickly put together with the crepes made ahead and shrimp bought already cooked.

In a blender or food processor, combine all crepe ingredients. Blend until batter is smooth. Cover and refrigerate for 1 hour.

Lightly oil a 6-inch skillet or crepe pan, or spray with nonstick cooking spray, and heat over medium heat. Stir the batter and pour 2 tablespoons into the pan. Cook about 1 minute, or until set. Turn and cook the other side about 45 seconds. Transfer to a sheet of parchment. Do not stack warm crepes. Use immediately. Or, stack cooled crepes and wrap them in both plastic wrap and an airtight plastic bag; refrigerate for up to 5 days or freeze for up to 2 months.

Heat oven to 425°F. In a large skillet, heat the butter and oil over medium-high heat. Add the garam masala or curry powder and cook, stirring, for 1 minute, or until fragrant. Add the wine and mint and cook, stirring, for 2 minutes, or until liquid is reduced slightly. Remove from the heat and stir in the shrimp, cheese, salt, and pepper.

Divide the filling between the crepes. Roll each one up and place seam side down in a shallow baking dish lightly coated with nonstick cooking spray. Bake for 10 minutes, or until the crepes are crisp. Serve with ¼ cup puréed peppers atop each serving.
Yield: 4 servings (25 unfilled crepes)

CREPES

- **1 cup unbleached or all-purpose flour**
- **¾ cup water**
- **⅔ cup milk**
- **3 large eggs, or ¾ cup egg substitute**
- **2 tablespoons canola oil**
- **¼ teaspoon salt**

FILLING

- **2 tablespoons butter**
- **2 tablespoons canola oil**
- **1 tablespoon garam masala or curry powder**
- **¼ cup dry white wine**
- **¼ cup finely sliced fresh mint leaves**
- **1 pound small or medium shrimp, peeled, deveined, and cooked**
- **1 cup low-fat or nonfat ricotta cheese**
- **½ teaspoon salt**
- **¼ teaspoon ground black pepper**
- **8 crepes, thawed if frozen**
- **1 cup puréed Roasted Red Bell Peppers (see recipe)**

ROASTED RED BELL PEPPERS

Hold a sweet red bell pepper over an open gas flame or charcoal fire, or place under a broiler. Turn until all sides are blackened. Put the pepper into a paper bag, close, and let cool for about 15 to 20 minutes. Remove and peel, cut in half, and remove stem and seeds. Slice into ¼-inch or ½-inch strips. Use immediately or store in the refrigerator covered with olive or canola oil.

To serve roasted peppers as an appetizer, combine 2 sliced roasted peppers with 1 minced garlic clove, 2 tablespoons extra-virgin olive oil, and 1 teaspoon minced basil or marjoram. Toss and let marinate for 1 hour at room temperature before serving.

CHILLED FISH STEAKS WITH FENNEL-BOURBON SAUCE

Fennel

FENNEL HAS BEEN grown since ancient times when Greek athletes ate it for strength and improved performance. Its botanical name, *Foeniculum*, is derived from the Latin word *foenum*, or "hay."

With a delicate, elusive taste reminiscent of anise and parsley, the sweetly fragrant leaves of fennel transform vegetables, seafood, soups, salads, and other dishes into epicurean fare. Be sure to try fish grilled with fennel leaves surrounding it and the stalks tossed onto the fire. Use the stronger-flavored seeds of fennel with stews, sausages, vegetables, meats, pickles, breads, liqueurs, and desserts.

Eating a few fennel seeds before a meal will help curb your appetite, and chewing a few afterwards will aid digestion. Tea brewed from the leaves or seeds will serve the same purposes. Fennel leaves are high in calcium, iron, potasssium, and vitamins A and C.

Lightly fried, then chilled and served with an unusually flavored sauce of fennel and bourbon, this dish is a superb choice for a summer luncheon or picnic.

- 4 haddock or halibut steaks (about 6 ounces each)
  Unbleached or all-purpose flour seasoned with salt and pepper for dredging
- 2 tablespoons canola oil
- ½ cup thinly sliced shallots
- 1 garlic clove, minced
- 1 pound tomatoes peeled, seeded, and chopped
- ⅓ cup minced fresh fennel leaves
- ½ cup dry vermouth
- ¼ cup water
- 1 tablespoon tomato paste
- ¼ teaspoon hot red pepper sauce
- 2 tablespoons bourbon
  Arugula or watercress leaves
  Minced parsley

Put the seasoned flour in a shallow dish and dredge each fish steak in the flour, shaking off the excess. In a large skillet, heat the oil over medium-high heat until hot but not smoking. Sauté the fish until lightly browned on both sides. Transfer the fish with a slotted spatula to paper towels to drain.

Add shallots to the skillet and cook, stirring occasionally, for about 2 minutes, or until soft and golden. Stir in garlic and cook, stirring, for 30 seconds. Add tomatoes and cook, stirring, for 3 minutes. Stir in fennel, vermouth, water, tomato paste, and hot pepper sauce. Reduce heat to low, partially cover, and simmer for 10 minutes.

Return the fish to the skillet. Warm the bourbon in a small saucepan and ignite. Immediately pour flaming liquid over the fish. Simmer about 3 minutes, or until fish is just cooked through. Chill fish in the sauce.

To serve, line a serving platter with stemmed arugula or watercress and arrange the fish on top. Spoon sauce over the top. Sprinkle with minced parsley.
Yield: 4 servings

ZESTY FISH STEW

Robust and hearty, this stew capitalizes on some of the most aromatic and spicy herbs. Although the ingredient list is long, the time involved is not.

Combine the tomatoes, onion, parsley, 2 tablespoons cilantro, thyme, garlic, chile pepper, lime juice, oil, salt, and pepper in a food processor fitted with a metal blade. Process until smooth. Place fish and shrimp in a nonreactive bowl and pour the processed mixture over the top. Cover and refrigerate for 1 hour.

Place seafood mixture in a large saucepan over medium heat. Stir in the bell peppers and stock or other liquid. Bring to a boil, then lower the heat and simmer for about 10 minutes, or until the seafood is cooked through. Stir in orange zest. Serve immediately over hot rice, sprinkled with the remaining 2 tablespoons cilantro.

Yield: 8 servings

- **2 pounds tomatoes, peeled, seeded, and chopped**
- **1½ cups chopped yellow onions**
- **¼ cup minced fresh parsley leaves**
- **¼ cup minced fresh cilantro leaves**
- **2 tablespoons minced fresh thyme leaves**
- **3 garlic cloves, minced**
- **1 serrano, habanero, or other hot chile pepper, cored, seeded, and minced**
- **¼ cup lime juice**
- **2 tablespoons canola oil**
- **½ teaspoon salt**
- **¼ teaspoon ground black pepper**
- **2 pounds boneless fish fillets of any firm, white fish, skinned and cut into 2-inch pieces**
- **1 pound small shrimp, peeled, tailed, and deveined**
- **2 red bell peppers, cored, seeded, and diced**
- **1 cup fish stock, bottled clam juice, vegetable stock or broth, or water**
- **2 tablespoons minced orange zest**
- **Hot cooked rice**

MONKFISH ROASTED WITH GARLIC, SHALLOTS, AND ROSEMARY

½ cup unbleached or all-purpose
   flour
½ teaspoon salt
¼ teaspoon ground black pepper
3 tablespoons canola oil
   Six 5- to 6-ounce monkfish fillets
10 garlic cloves, peeled and
   crushed
¼ pound shallots, peeled and
   crushed
   Five 4-inch rosemary sprigs
½ cup dry white wine

Firm, meaty monkfish is also known as angler or poor man's lobster. Its natural, rich succulence is embellished when simply prepared with garlic, shallots, and rosemary.

Preheat oven to 375°F. Combine the flour, salt, and pepper in a shallow pan and dredge the monkfish in the mixture, shaking off the excess.

In an ovenproof pan just large enough to hold the fish in a single layer, heat the oil over high heat. Add the fish and shake the pan to be sure the fish doesn't stick. Lower the heat to medium-high and sauté until one side is golden brown. Turn the fish to its second side and add the garlic, shallots, and rosemary. When that side is golden turn the pieces to the third side and cook until golden brown. Flip the fish back to the first side and put the pan in the preheated oven for 7 minutes.

Sprinkle the wine over the fish and continue cooking for about 5 more minutes. The fish is done when the ribbed muscles at the thick end can be separated easily. Remove the fish from the pan and keep warm on a platter. Pour the juices through a strainer into a small bowl. Serve the monkfish sliced like a roast, with the pan juices. *Yield: 6 servings*

Across the world, wherever it grows, a sprig of Rosemary is never just a fragrant green herb, but a bit of human history in one's hands.

— Dorothy Bovee Jones, *The Herbarist*, 1961

Chicken Breast Rolls with Herbed Ricotta Stuffing (page 76) ▶

Poultry & Meat
Main Courses

CHICKEN BREAST ROLLS WITH HERBED RICOTTA STUFFING

8 chicken breast halves (about 6 to 8 ounces each), skinless and boneless
16 ounces low-fat or nonfat ricotta cheese
½ cup dry breadcrumbs
2 tablespoons small capers, drained
1 tablespoon minced garlic
2 teaspoons minced fresh basil leaves
1 teaspoon minced fresh oregano leaves
½ teaspoon salt
¼ teaspoon ground white pepper
½ teaspoon hot red pepper sauce
1 cup dry white wine
Paprika

One of the benefits of using herbs in cooking is that they can compensate for the loss of flavor in low-fat dishes. These chicken rolls are a perfect example. Try using your own favorite herb combinations as well as basil and oregano.

Heat oven to 350ºF. Flatten each chicken breast by placing it between two sheets of wax paper and pounding it with a mallet or rolling pin until it is ¼-inch thick.

Combine ricotta, breadcrumbs, capers, garlic, basil, oregano, salt, pepper, and hot red pepper sauce in a medium-sized bowl.

Divide the ricotta mixture into 8 portions (about 3 tablespoons each) and spread a portion on a flattened chicken breast, keeping it about ¼ inch from the edges. Starting at one of the shorter sides, roll it up. Run a toothpick through and place seam side down in a buttered shallow casserole or baking dish. Repeat with each breast. Pour on the wine. Dust with paprika. Bake for 30 minutes, until lightly browned.

Yield: 4 to 6 servings

Young plants of oregano and other herbs planted in a decorative container in a brightly lit kitchen can provide clippings of fresh herbs for weeks.

CHICKEN RAGOUT WITH OLIVES, OREGANO, AND CILANTRO

.... ❖ ....

Derived from a French word meaning "to stimulate the appetite," this robust and hearty baked chicken casserole is a well-seasoned stew that needs little more than crusty bread and salad to make a feast. Be sure the oregano has a good flavor. For a milder taste, substitute marjoram. Oil-cured olives can be found at specialty food markets.

Heat oven to 350ºF. Combine the onions, tomatoes, garlic, olives, and oregano in a large bowl. Combine the flour and pepper in a flat pan or dish. Dredge the chicken breasts in the flour mixture. Shake off the excess.

In a large, heavy-bottomed nonstick skillet, heat the oil over medium heat. Add the dredged chicken breasts in a single layer, pressing down gently on each one to brown the entire surface. Cook each side about 4 minutes, or until golden brown. Remove the chicken breasts to a baking dish large enough the hold all the chicken in one layer.

Put the tomato mixture in the skillet and cook, stirring occasionally, about 10 minutes, until vegetables are soft. Combine red and white wines, port, and vinegar in a small saucepan. Cook over medium-high heat until reduced to 1 cup.

Spread the tomato mixture over chicken breasts and pour on the reduced liquid. Bake for 30 minutes, or until the chicken is tender.

Remove the chicken breasts to a platter. Stir the cilantro and lemon juice into the sauce and pour over the chicken. Serve immediately.
Yield: 8 servings

3 cups chopped yellow onions
2 pounds tomatoes, peeled, seeded, and chopped
6 garlic cloves, peeled and crushed
½ pound oil-cured black olives, pitted and chopped
½ cup fresh oregano leaves
½ cup unbleached or all-purpose flour
½ teaspoon ground black pepper
8 chicken breast halves (6 to 8 ounces each), boneless and skinless
¼ cup canola oil
⅔ cup dry red wine
⅔ cup dry white wine
¼ cup dry port
2 tablespoons red wine vinegar
½ cup fresh cilantro leaves
¼ cup lemon juice

CILANTRO RELISH

To hold to tradition, try this relish, or more accurately, sambal, with a spicy curry. But why not enjoy its unique flavor with grilled, poached, or baked fish or poultry.

To prepare, combine coconut milk, cilantro leaves, garlic , ginger-root, chile peppers, lime juice, salt, brown sugar, and cumin in a blender or food processor. Store in a covered container in the refrigerator for up to 3 weeks.

1 cup coconut milk, regular or low-fat
1 cup fresh cilantro leaves
2 garlic cloves, peeled
One ½-inch piece fresh ginger-root, peeled
2 small green chile peppers
⅓ cup lime juice
½ teaspoon salt
1 teaspoon brown sugar
1 teaspoon ground cumin

Southwestern Grilled Chicken Salad with Anaheim Chiles

Chile Pepper

CHILE PEPPERS NOT ONLY have flavor benefits, they also have a high vitamin C content as well as significant amounts of vitamins A and B-complex, calcium, phosphorus, iron, and protein. Their medicinal value ranges from relieving painful joints and sprains to soothing toothaches, sore throats, fevers, nausea, and indigestion. They also increase blood flow.

Although the milder chile peppers fall more into the vegetable category, the hotter ones are most often used in the smaller quantities associated with herbs. Unlike many herbs, chile peppers are similar in taste whether used fresh or dried. Thin-skinned chile peppers, such as 'Cayenne', are most often used dried, although fresh works just as well. Thick-skinned chile peppers, such as 'Anaheim', are usually used fresh; roasting particularly enhances their flavor.

Chili powder is not to be confused with chile peppers. The commercially available powder is actually a blend of various chile peppers, herbs, and spices.

Anaheim chiles are also known as California or long green chiles. Usually about 6 inches long and 2 inches or so in diameter, they are only mildly hot. Unless the corn is absolutely fresh and tender, it's best to boil it for 3 minutes in water with a tablespoon each of salt and sugar added.

- 4 chicken breast halves (6 to 8 ounces each), skinless and boneless
- 3 tablespoons canola oil
- ¼ cup low-fat or reduced-calorie mayonnaise
- 2 tablespoons red wine vinegar
- 1 tablespoon commercial chili powder
- 3 green Anaheim chiles
- 1 pound romaine lettuce, washed and trimmed
- ⅔ pound jicama, peeled and julienned
- Kernels from 4 medium ears of sweet corn, or 2 cups frozen corn, cooked
- 3 medium ripe tomatoes (about 1 pound), cored and cut into wedges
- ½ cup fresh cilantro leaves

Put the chicken breasts in a shallow dish large enough to hold them in a single layer, and pour the oil over the top, turning to coat. Let stand for 30 minutes.

Combine the mayonnaise, red wine vinegar, and chili powder in a small bowl.

Preheat the broiler. Roast the chile peppers under the broiler, turning as each side blackens. When blackened all over, remove from oven, put hot chiles in a paper bag, close it, and let them steam. When cooled, peel the chiles, remove the stems, scrape out the seeds, and cut into 1-inch pieces. Set aside.

Tear the romaine leaves into bite-sized pieces and put them in a large bowl. Add the jicama, corn kernels, roasted chiles, tomatoes, and cilantro to the lettuce.

Prepare the grill. Grill the chicken until done, or about 4 minutes on each side.

Pour the chili mayonnaise over the romaine and vegetables and toss gently but thoroughly. Divide among four plates. Slice the chicken and put it on top.

Yield: 4 servings

HERB-ROASTED CORNISH HENS

Here's an extremely simple, basic recipe on which you can really turn your creativity loose! With a variety of pantry staples and an assortment of fresh herbs, any number of ethnic flavors can be readily achieved. For those so inclined, use butter instead of oil for basting. Or, use a mixture of soy sauce, sherry or rice wine, and sesame oil with basil and lemongrass or ginger. The herbs can also be combined with grainy or Dijon-style mustard. Lime, ginger, sage, cumin, and allspice lend a Caribbean flavor. Fresh basil combined with minced sun-dried tomatoes and goat cheese and stuffed under the breast skin yields a savory tang.

4 Cornish hens (about 1 pound each)
Eight 3-inch fresh herb sprigs
6 garlic cloves, thinly sliced
2 tablespoons minced fresh herb leaves or flowers, such as thyme, rosemary, and marjoram
1 teaspoon salt
½ teaspoon ground black pepper
1 lemon
2 tablespoons olive oil
1 cup vegetable stock, canned vegetable broth, or white wine

Heat oven to 400°F. Insert two herb sprigs into the cavities of each hen. In a small bowl, combine garlic, herbs, salt, and pepper. With your fingers, loosen the breast skin of each hen. Spread one-fourth of the herb mixture under the skin of each. Rub the outside of the hens with a piece of cut lemon, brush with olive oil, then rub the remainder of the herb mixture over the skin. Put the hens, not touching, in a shallow pan. Roast them, basting every 15 minutes with stock, broth, or wine. After 15 minutes, reduce the heat to 300°F and cook another 30 to 40 minutes, or until the juices run clear when a small slit is made in the upper thigh.
Yield: 4 to 8 servings

*The thyme strong scented
  'neath our feet,
The Marjoram beds so
  doubly sweet,
And pennyroyal's creeping
  twine
These, each succeeding each
  one thine.*

— from Mrs. C. F. Leyel's *Herbal Delights*

Roast Duck with Sage and Pine Nut Stuffing

One 2-inch piece fresh ginger-
    root, peeled and thinly sliced
½ cup honey
2 tablespoons soy sauce
¼ cup orange marmalade
    One 4-pound duck, giblets
    removed
½ cup pine nuts
½ cup long grain white rice
¾ pound apples, peeled, cored,
    and chopped
½ teaspoon salt
1 bay leaf
1 cup boiling water
½ cup minced fresh sage leaves
½ teaspoon ground black pepper
¼ teaspoon ground cloves
¼ teaspoon ground allspice
¼ teaspoon ground nutmeg
1 tablespoon canola oil

One of the most underused of herbs, sage has long played a major role in German cooking, especially with sausages, goose, and duck. Besides its affinity in terms of flavor, sage's ability to aid digestion certainly has benefits with fat-rich foods. In addition to inhibiting the oxidation of fats, sage is rich in vitamins A and C.

Combine the ginger, honey, soy sauce, and marmalade in a shallow bowl large enough to hold the duck. Brush the duck with the mixture and let it stand in the marinade for 30 minutes. Brush the duck again, turn it over, and let it stand for another 30 minutes.

Heat oven to 400°F. Put the pine nuts in a single layer in a baking pan and toast, stirring occasionally, for about 5 minutes, or until golden.

Combine the rice, apples, salt, bay leaf, and boiling water in a small saucepan. Place over medium-low heat, cover, and simmer for about 20 minutes, or until rice is tender.

Combine the rice mixture, toasted pine nuts, sage, pepper, cloves, allspice, and nutmeg in a large bowl.

Fold under the large flap of skin at the duck's neck, then bend the wings over the flap to keep it sealed. Salt and pepper the body cavity inside, then stuff with the rice–pine nut mixture. Tie the legs together with kitchen string to close the cavity.

Put the duck in a roasting pan just big enough to hold it. Roast for 20 minutes. Prick the skin gently with the tines of a fork — go deep enough to reach the fat layer but not into the meat. Baste the duck with any remaining soy-honey glaze. Reduce the heat to 350°F and cook for about 40 minutes more, or until the duck is medium-rare. Cut into four pieces and serve with the stuffing.

Yield: 2 to 3 servings

Sage

GRILLED RIB-EYE STEAK WITH CUMIN AND OREGANO

This unusual combination of herbs and bourbon makes a marinade that accentuates the flavor of grilled steak.

Combine cumin, oregano, bourbon, olive oil, and black pepper in a mortar and pestle or blender until a smooth paste is formed. Rub onto both sides of the steaks. Let sit for 1 hour at room temperature, or overnight, covered, in the refrigerator.

Prepare a grill or heat the oven broiler. Coat the grill or broiler pan with nonstick cooking spray. Cook the steaks on one side until a nice, deep-brown crust forms. Turn and finish cooking to medium-rare.
Yield: 4 servings

2 tablespoons ground cumin
    seeds
½ cup fresh oregano leaves
4 teaspoons bourbon
2 tablespoons olive oil
1½ teaspoons ground black pepper
4 rib-eye steaks, 1 inch thick
    (about 8 ounces each)

ARUGULA BURGERS

The peppery taste of arugula accents the flavor of the beef, and the bulgur keeps the lean meat moist. Tangy, fresh goat cheese is the surprise inside.

In a medium-sized bowl, combine bulgur with hot water. Let stand for 30 minutes, or until water is absorbed and bulgur is tender.

Prepare a grill or heat the oven broiler. Add beef, arugula, salt, and pepper to the bulgur. Mix thoroughly but with as little stirring as possible. Shape the mixture into eight thin patties. Divide and sprinkle the cheese on four of the patties. Top with the remaining patties and seal the edges.

Coat the grill or broiler pan with nonstick cooking spray. Cook the burgers about 5 minutes on each side, or until cooked through. Serve on buns with fresh arugula.

Variation: Fresh watercress may be substituted for the arugula. Try other cheeses as well.
Yield: 4 servings

⅓ cup bulgur
½ cup hot water
¾ pound lean ground beef
¾ cup coarsely chopped fresh
    arugula, stems removed
½ teaspoon salt
¼ teaspoon ground black pepper
¼ cup crumbled fresh goat cheese
8 hamburger buns
    Fresh arugula

FILET OF BEEF WITH THYME AND MADEIRA SAUCE

3 tablespoons whole black peppercorns
2 teaspoons fresh rosemary leaves
6 garlic cloves, peeled
1 tablespoon salt
3 tablespoons olive oil
One 2½- to 3-pound filet mignon, trimmed of fat
Ten 4-inch sprigs fresh thyme
½ pound carrots, chopped
1 stalk celery, cut in ½-inch slices
¼ cup chopped shallots
1 cup dry Madeira
½ cup dry red wine
1 tablespoon sherry vinegar
6 ounces beef stock or canned beef broth

One of the classic food combinations is beef and thyme. The juicy tenderness of filet mignon is perfectly paired with a very dry, delicate Madeira and the thyme. Among the best thymes for cooking are those labeled English and French.

Grind the peppercorns and rosemary in a blender until they are mostly pulverized; a few small chunks are fine. Add the garlic and salt, and process. Add 2 tablespoons of oil in a thin, slow stream, blending until the mixture is a spreadable paste. Rub the mixture all over the filet, then let the meat stand for 2 hours at room temperature.

Heat oven to 350°F. Scrape most of the spice rub off the filet, saving ½ teaspoon. Heat the remaining tablespoon of oil in an ovenproof skillet over high heat and brown the filet mignon on all sides. Because of the pepper in the rub, the crust that forms will be almost black. When the meat is seared on all sides, put the skillet in the oven and cook for 25 to 30 minutes, depending on the desired doneness.

Remove the filet and wrap loosely in foil. Scrape any burned pieces out of the skillet and add the thyme, carrots, celery, and shallots. Cook over medium heat, stirring, for 3 minutes, or until thyme is fragrant. Stir in Madeira, wine, vinegar, and stock or broth. Reduce the liquid to 1 cup. Add any juice that has accumulated in the foil, and season with the reserved pepper rub. Strain the sauce and serve immediately with the sliced filet.

Yield: 8 servings

*What time the mighty moon
Was gathering light
Love paced the thymy plots
Of Paradise*

— Alfred, Lord Tennyson

Thyme

THERE ARE MANY legends and uses associated with thyme:

- Thyme was burned in ancient Greek temples as incense.
- Roman soldiers bathed in thyme water to increase their courage.
- Medieval English ladies often presented their knights with sprigs of thyme or a thyme-embroidered favor to inspire them with courage.
- On St. Agnes Eve, young girls placed sprigs of thyme and rosemary in their shoes, believing this would bring them a vision of the man they would marry.
- Because thyme was long believed to be beloved by fairies, people set aside a corner of their gardens to grow a patch of thyme solely for them.
- Thyme was thought to prevent nightmares, soothe nerves, and cure shyness.
- As recently as World War I, the essential oil of thyme was used to treat wounds owing to its antiseptic qualities. (Check your mouthwash bottle for thymol!)
- An infusion of thyme disinfects burns and cuts; taken internally, it is used for treating colds and sore throats.
- Dried sprigs of thyme placed in a closet or bureau repel moths.
- An infusion of thyme is an excellent conditioner for dark hair.
- Thyme in bathwater relieves aches and softens skin.

GRILLED LAMB CHOPS WITH ORANGE-CHIVE SAUCE

············· ❖ ·············

SAUCE

- 1 tablespoon canola oil
- ½ cup chopped shallots
- ¼ cup brandy
- 2 tablespoons minced fresh chives
- 1 cup orange juice
- 3 tablespoons raisins
- ½ cup water
- 2 tablespoons arrowroot

CHOPS

- 12 loin lamb chops, each about ¾-inch thick (about 2 pounds)
- ¼ cup orange juice
- ¼ cup canola oil
- 2 tablespoons minced fresh chives
- ½ teaspoon ground black pepper

The delicate yet distinctly onion-like flavor of chives and shallots is the cornerstone of this simple sauce for grilled lamb chops.

To prepare the sauce, heat the oil in a small skillet over medium heat. Add the shallots and cook, stirring, for about 4 minutes, or until soft. Add the brandy and chives and cook until almost all the liquid has evaporated. Add the orange juice and simmer until reduced by half. Add the raisins and cook for 3 minutes, or until plump. Mix the water and arrowroot in a small bowl and stir into the skillet. Stirring constantly, cook until the sauce is thickened. Keep warm.

Prepare grill or heat the oven broiler. Combine orange juice, oil, chives, and pepper in a small bowl. Brush both sides of each lamb chop with the mixture, and grill or broil for about 4 minutes on each side until medium-rare. Serve with the sauce.

Yield: 6 servings

LAMB STEW WITH ROSEMARY AND SAGE

◆

Both rosemary and sage have a camphorous aspect to their flavor, which proves to be an admirable complement to lamb.

  1 tablespoon canola oil
1½ pounds boneless lamb, cut into 1½-inch cubes
  1 tablespoon minced fresh rosemary leaves
  1 tablespoon minced fresh sage leaves
  1 garlic clove, minced
  2 teaspoons unbleached or all-purpose flour
  ⅓ cup red wine–herb vinegar
  ⅔ cup vegetable stock, or canned vegetable broth
  2 anchovy fillets, minced
  2 tablespoons minced fresh parsley leaves

Heat the oil in a large skillet over medium heat. Add lamb and cook, stirring, until the meat is browned on all sides. Add rosemary, sage, and garlic and cook, stirring occasionally, for 3 minutes. Sprinkle with flour, stir, and cook for 1 minute. Slowly add vinegar and stock or broth, and stir well. Cover and reduce heat to low. Simmer for 40 minutes, or until the meat is tender. Mix a little of the hot liquid with the anchovies, then stir into the stew. Simmer for 5 minutes, uncovered. Transfer to a serving dish and sprinkle with parsley.
Yield: 4 servings

MINT SAUCE

Instead of mint jelly, try this traditional English tart-sweet sauce with lamb, using any of the strong-flavored spearmints. Don't just use it with lamb, though. Try it with other grilled meats, poached fish or cold shellfish, mixed with mayonnaise, or with salads or salad dressings.

In a small nonreactive saucepan, combine vinegar with sugar or honey. Cook over medium heat, stirring, until sugar or honey is dissolved. Remove from heat and stir in spearmint. Cover and steep for several hours. Refrigerated, the sauce will keep for several weeks.

Other herbs to substitute for mint include anise hyssop, chervil, fennel, lemon verbena, and tarragon.

Rosemary

GROWN AND USED for centuries, rosemary was a strewing herb and charm to ward off evil. Ancient Greek students wore rosemary during exams to focus their minds and sharpen their memories. Rosemary was popular with the Tudors and Elizabethans in wedding garlands, where it represented fidelity. It also was used for incense, for warding off fevers, and for tossing into graves at funerals as a token of remembrance.

The resinous flavor and scent of rosemary makes a natural pairing with lamb, poultry, and pork. Add it to soups and stews or use it to flavor peas, beans, and cauliflower as well as breads, scones, muffins, herb butters, and vinegars. Rosemary makes a wonderful jelly to serve with roast meats. Or, try it infused with chilled white wine or hot mulled cider or wine.

½ cup vinegar
2 tablespoons white or brown
    sugar or 1 tablespoon honey
1 cup minced fresh spearmint
    leaves

ROAST PORK LOIN STUFFED WITH DRIED APRICOTS, SHALLOTS, AND SAGE

.... ❖ ....

4 tablespoons canola oil
1 pound dried apricots, cut into
  ¼-inch pieces
2 tablespoons chopped shallots
4 scallions, cut into ¼-inch slices
⅓ cup raisins
1 tablespoon chopped fresh sage
  leaves
½ cup brandy
2 cups orange juice
1½ cups coarse dry breadcrumbs
2 large eggs, lightly beaten, or
  ½ cup egg substitute
4- to 5-pound boneless pork
  loin, trimmed

The musky flavor of fresh sage offsets the sweetness of the fruit, yielding a mélange that perfectly accents the pork. This is an elegant main course that also is great at room temperature, perhaps for a picnic.

Heat oven to 500°F. Heat 2 tablespoons canola oil in a skillet over medium-high heat and stir in the apricots, shallots, scallions, raisins, and sage. Cook for about 2 minutes, or until the sage is fragrant. Stir in the brandy and simmer for 1 minute. Stir in 1 cup orange juice, bring to a boil, lower heat to medium, and reduce liquid by one-third. Remove from the heat and stir in the breadcrumbs. Let cool. Stir in the eggs.

Cut the pork loin in half lengthwise, leaving one side attached. Fold open and cut out a trough about 1 inch deep and 2 inches wide in the center of each half. Fill the troughs with the breadcrumb mixture. Fold the two halves together and tie with kitchen string.

Heat the remaining 2 tablespoons oil in a large ovenproof skillet or roasting pan over high heat. Add the pork loin and brown on all sides. Pour in remaining 1 cup orange juice. Transfer to oven and cook for 10 minutes. Reduce heat to 350°F. Basting every 20 minutes, cook for 1½ hours. Remove from oven and let stand for 10 minutes. Cut into 1-inch slices and serve with the pan juices.
Yield: 8 to 10 servings

How can a man grow old who has sage in his garden?

— Chinese proverb

Sage

A NATIVE OF THE northern Mediterranean coast, sage has long been associated with wisdom, longevity, and even immortality. The genus name *Salvia* is derived from the Latin *salvere*, which means "to be in good health," "to cure," or "salvation." The Romans revered sage, gathering it only through elaborate ceremony.

Although there are more than 750 varieties of sage, common sage (*Salvia officinalis*) remains the culinary variety of choice. There is a type with large, broad leaves and another with small leaves and dwarf growth. Also meriting attention is golden sage (*S. officinalis* 'Aurea'), with a mild flavor and showy golden leaves. Purple sage (*S. o.* 'Purpurea') boasts a delightful flavor and aroma. The deep purple leaves are striking as a garnish and quite lovely in tea as well as in cooking. There is also a triple-variegated common sage, with leaves of pink, cream, and green, that is favored for its decorative quality.

GRILLED PORK CHOPS WITH CRANBERRY-BERGAMOT SAUCE

·· ❖ ··

Four 6-ounce boneless pork chops, 1 inch thick
Canola oil or nonstick cooking spray

SAUCE

1 tablespoon canola oil
¼ cup minced shallots
¾ cup orange juice
¼ cup dried cranberries
¼ cup minced fresh bergamot leaves
2 tablespoons orange liqueur
½ teaspoon orange zest
1 tablespoon arrowroot powder
1 tablespoon water
Fresh bergamot flowers

Bergamot, also known as bee balm, Monardo, and Oswego tea, is one of the few native American herbs and edible flowers. With a flavor variously described as citrusy, minty, sweet, and hot, bergamot leaves and flowers are most often used in breads, drinks, and desserts. When combined with tart cranberries, the bergamot is an ideal foil for grilled pork.

While preparing the sauce, heat the grill or oven broiler. Brush the pork chops with canola oil or nonstick cooking spray, and cook for about 5 minutes on each side, or until done.

To prepare the sauce, heat the oil in a saucepan over medium heat. Add the shallots and cook, stirring occasionally, for 2 minutes, or until soft. Stir in the orange juice, cranberries, bergamot, liqueur, and zest and simmer for 3 minutes, or until cranberries are soft.

Serve each pork chop with some of the sauce. Garnish with fresh bergamot flower petals, if available.

Yield: 4 servings

HORSERADISH SAUCE

···

½ cup grated horseradish root (peeled)
3 tablespoons vinegar
½ teaspoon salt

Pungent horseradish root, grated and stored in vinegar, is the basic ingredient in a range of sauces ideal for roasted or boiled beef, roasted pork, and cold cut sandwiches. You might even want to try it with duck or goose.

To prepare, combine grated horseradish root with vinegar and salt. Store in a covered jar in the refrigerator.

To use, stir some of the horseradish into sour cream, applesauce, or berry jelly.

For a variation, substitute fresh gingerroot for the horseradish root.

Garden Vegetables Grilled on a Rosemary Skewer (page 90) ▶

Vegetables, Grains & Beans

Garden Vegetables Grilled on a Rosemary Skewer

❖

5 tablespoons olive oil
12 baby summer squash, such as zucchini, yellow crookneck, or patty pan
12 cherry or pear tomatoes
12 baby eggplants or 1-inch cubes of eggplant
12 baby leeks or 1-inch sections of leek
Six 12-inch rosemary stems, stripped and soaked in water for 1 hour

The essence of rosemary works its way from the inside out on grilled vegetables skewered on the stems of this resinous herb. Without artifice, the result is the essence of summer.

Toss all the vegetables with 4 tablespoons of the olive oil in a large bowl. Let stand for 1 hour.

Divide the vegetables into six portions and alternate them on the rosemary-stem skewers. Skewer the leeks from the outside of the skin, not through the cut center. Salt and pepper the vegetables, if desired.

Prepare the grill. Cook the vegetables about 10 minutes, or until they are tender, turning and brushing them with additional olive oil as necessary. Serve immediately.

Yield: 6 servings

Oven-Roasted Vegetables with Herbs

❖

3 sweet potatoes, peeled and cut into 1-inch pieces
3 carrots, halved crosswise, then lengthwise
2 onions, peeled and cut into 8 wedges
1 garlic head, separated into cloves, peeled
¼ cup minced fresh rosemary leaves
¼ cup minced fresh thyme leaves
3 tablespoons olive oil

This is comfort food in every sense. Not only are roasted vegetables easy to prepare, but they also are as satisfying as seeing an old friend. Besides the ingredients listed, consider white potatoes, winter squash, or sage. "Soft" vegetables such as summer squash or mushrooms also roast well, but need only 30 minutes to cook.

Heat oven to 400°F. In a large bowl, toss together sweet potatoes, carrots, onion, garlic, rosemary, and thyme. Drizzle oil over the top and toss again. Spread mixture on a large baking sheet and bake about 1 hour, or until golden and tender, stirring occasionally. Season with salt and pepper, if desired. Transfer to a platter and serve.

Yield: 6 servings

STEAMED SUMMER SQUASH AND CARROTS WITH LEMON HERBS

.... ❖ ....

Create culinary alchemy with lemon-flavored herbs such as lemon thyme, lemon basil, lemon verbena, and lemon balm. Just as real lemons enhance the flavor of foods, so do these herbs, with the bonus of their own distinctive flavor.

In a large saucepan fitted with a collapsible vegetable steamer, bring 1 inch of water to a boil. Steam the carrots, covered, for 2 minutes. Add summer squash, replace cover, and steam for about 5 minutes, or until the vegetables are tender crisp.

Heat oil or butter in a large skillet over medium heat. Stir in cooked vegetables, sherry or vinegar, lemon thyme, lemon verbena, lemon basil, salt, and pepper. Cook, stirring, for about 2 minutes, or until hot. Serve immediately.
Yield: 4 servings

½ pound carrots, cut into julienne strips
⅔ pound summer squash, cut into julienne strips
1 tablespoon canola oil or butter
1 tablespoon sherry or balsamic vinegar
1 teaspoon chopped fresh lemon thyme leaves
1 teaspoon chopped fresh lemon verbena leaves
1 teaspoon chopped fresh lemon basil leaves
¼ teaspoon salt
⅛ teaspoon ground black pepper

BATTER-FRIED FLOWERS

.... ❖ ....

Daylily or squash blossoms dipped in batter and lightly browned provide an unusual and delicious side dish. Pick the flowers just as they open, cut off the base, and flatten the bloom before dipping in the batter.

To make the batter, soften the minced garlic in the tablespoon of canola oil. Whisk together the garlic, eggs or egg substitute, flour, salt and pepper, and nutmeg. If batter is too thick, whisk in a teaspoon or so of milk. Dip each flower in the batter, then sauté in the remaining canola oil until golden. Serve immediately.

Daylily or squash blossoms
1 garlic clove minced
1 tablespoon plus ¼ cup canola oil
3 large eggs, or ¾ cup egg substitute
½ cup flour
Salt and pepper, to taste
Dash of nutmeg

Tomatoes and Olives with Herbs

❖

1 tablespoon olive oil
2 tablespoons chopped fresh
   parsley leaves
4 garlic cloves, minced
½ cup drained kalamata olives,
   pitted and chopped
½ cup drained, pitted, and
   chopped imported green
   olives
2 pounds tomatoes, cored and
   quartered
2 tablespoons chopped fresh
   basil leaves
1 tablespoon chopped fresh
   chives
½ teaspoon ground black pepper

Sun-ripened tomatoes are one of summer's glories. A quick cooking and simple pairing with olives, garlic, parsley, basil, and chives brings out their voluptuous best.

Heat the oil in a large skillet over medium-high heat. Cook the parsley and garlic in the oil, stirring frequently, for about 2 minutes, or until garlic is golden. Do not let it brown. Reduce heat to medium. Stir in the olives. Cook, uncovered, for 3 minutes, stirring frequently. Add the tomatoes and cook, stirring, for about 2 minutes, or until the tomatoes are warm. Add the basil, chives, and pepper. Cook about 30 seconds, until the herbs are wilted and fragrant. Serve immediately.

Yield: 6 servings

Gratin of Fennel and Lovage

❖

2 tablespoons canola oil
½ pound quartered and cored
   fennel bulbs (fronds removed)
1 cup lovage stalks, cut into
   ½-inch slices
1¼ cups chopped yellow onions
¼ cup chopped fresh lovage
   leaves
½ cup dry white wine
½ cup vegetable stock or canned
   vegetable broth
½ cup heavy cream or evaporated
   skim milk
½ cup grated Parmesan cheese

Lore has it that lovage makes a potent love potion. Whatever the validity of such claims may be, lovage's strong celery-like flavor certainly goes well with the delicate anise flavor of fennel. The addition of onions, cream, and Parmesan works its own particular magic.

Heat oven to 350°F. In an ovenproof pan, heat the oil over medium-high heat. Add the fennel, lovage stalks, and onion and cook, stirring occasionally, about 8 minutes, or until soft. Add the lovage leaves and cook another 2 or 3 minutes, until they are wilted but still green. Add the wine and stock or broth and bring to a boil. Cover and bake for 1 hour, or until fennel is completely tender; then remove from the oven.

Increase oven temperature to 450°F. Drain off the excess liquid from the baked mixture. Combine the cream or evaporated milk and cheese and pour over the baked vegetables. Return to the oven and bake for 15 minutes.

Yield: 6 to 8 servings

CORN, BABY LIMA BEANS, AND TOMATOES WITH PARSLEY

❖

This is an uptown version of down-home succotash, a word that comes from the Narragansett Indians, meaning "boiled whole kernels of corn." Parsley, tomatoes, and wine are not normally included, but each adds to the quality of the dish. Flat-leaf parsley tends to have a better flavor, but use the curly-leaf type if that's all you have.

Heat the butter and oil in a large skillet over medium-high heat. Stir in the corn and cook, stirring constantly, for 1 minute. Add the wine and salt, and continue to cook for 5 to 7 minutes, or until most of the liquid is gone. Add the tomatoes, lima beans, and pepper. Cook, stirring occasionally, for another 3 minutes, or until beans are tender. Stir in the parsley and cook for 1 minute, or until parsley is wilted. Serve immediately.
Yield: 6 servings

1 tablespoon butter
1 tablespoon canola oil
   Kernels from 4 medium ears fresh corn (about 2 cups)
⅔ cup dry white wine
½ teaspoon salt
1 pound tomatoes, peeled, seeded, and diced
1 cup shelled fresh baby lima beans
¼ teaspoon ground black pepper
1 cup chopped fresh parsley leaves

. . . the beautiful verdure of this plant [parsley] forms an elegant garnishing to our dishes; it is the luxury of the soup-kettle; it adds to the delight of the most splendid dinners.

— Frances S. Osgood

CARROT-TURNIP-ROSEMARY TIMBALES

❖

2 cups finely chopped carrots
2 cups finely chopped turnips
Four 4-inch sprigs fresh
    rosemary
½ cup water
1 teaspoon salt
½ cup heavy cream or evaporated
    skim milk
½ cup milk
2 large eggs, lightly beaten, or
    ½ cup egg substitute
1 teaspoon white wine vinegar
½ teaspoon ground white pepper
¼ teaspoon ground nutmeg
Eight 1-inch sprigs fresh
    rosemary

If you don't have the special molds designed for timbales, individual custard or soufflé ramekins will suit the purpose. Whatever you use, don't let the simplicity of this dish fool you; the whole is much more than the sum of its parts.

Combine the carrots, turnips, 4-inch rosemary sprigs, water, and salt in a saucepan. Place over medium-high heat, bring to a boil, then cover and reduce heat to low. Simmer for 10 minutes, then remove lid and cook for another 20 minutes. Most of the moisture should be cooked away, but the carrots should still have their color; be sure the vegetables don't burn. Remove the rosemary sprigs, drain, and purée the vegetables in a food processor, blender, or food mill. Place the purée in an unbleached muslin towel and squeeze to extract all remaining moisture.

Heat oven to 350°F and place a pan containing 1 inch of hot water on the upper rack. Cut circles of baking parchment to fit the tops of the timbale molds or 6-ounce custard cups. Butter the molds or cups and the parchment.

Combine the cream or evaporated milk, milk, eggs or egg substitute, vinegar, white pepper, and nutmeg in a large bowl. Add the puréed vegetables and mix thoroughly. Pour into the prepared molds and cover each mold with the buttered parchment paper. Place the molds in the water bath in the oven. Cook for 45 minutes, until the centers of the custards just begin to spring back when lightly touched. Remove from the molds and serve immediately, garnished with a sprig of fresh rosemary.
Yield: 8 servings

*I plant Rosemary all over
the garden, so pleasant it
is to know that at every
few steps one may draw
the kindly branchlets
through one's hand, and
have the enjoyment of
their incomparable
incense; and I grow it
against walls, so that the
sun may draw out its
inexhaustible sweetness to
greet me as I pass . . .*

— Gertrude Jekyll

White Beans with Tomatoes, Thyme, Savory, and Tarragon

1 pound white kidney or Great
   Northern beans
¼ cup canola oil
3 cups chopped yellow onions
6 garlic cloves, crushed
1 bay leaf
   Five 4-inch sprigs fresh thyme
   Three 4-inch sprigs fresh savory
4 whole cloves
½ cup dry white wine
¼ cup white wine vinegar
2 tablespoons Worcestershire
   sauce
5 cups vegetable stock or canned
   vegetable broth
2½ pounds tomatoes, peeled,
   seeded, and chopped
3 tablespoons chopped fresh
   tarragon leaves
¼ cup lemon juice
1 teaspoon salt
½ teaspoon ground black pepper

Thyme and savory lend their rich, melodic flavors to a dish that is a perfect centerpiece to a meal of vegetables or a sturdy side dish to chicken or pork. For those without the time or inclination to cook dry beans, substitute 3 cans of drained, cooked beans; do not use extra water; and cook for about 30 minutes before adding the tomatoes.

Soak the dried beans for 12 hours in a large bowl of cold water that covers them by at least 4 inches. Change the water once, after 6 hours.

Heat the oil in a large saucepan over medium-high heat. Add the onions and garlic, and cook, stirring, for about 8 minutes, or until soft. Stir in the bay leaf, thyme, savory, and cloves, and cook for 2 to 3 more minutes, or until the herbs are fragrant. Add the beans, wine, vinegar, Worcestershire sauce, stock or broth, and enough water to cover the beans by 2 inches. Bring to a boil, skim off foam, and reduce heat to low. Cover and cook until beans are tender, or about 2 hours. Stir in the tomatoes, turn up heat to medium-high, and cook for 5 minutes, stirring occasionally. Add the tarragon and cook for 3 minutes. Add the lemon juice, salt, and pepper. Serve immediately. *Yield: 8 servings*

The Thymes are herbs of the classical world, plants of the old agriculture and the gods, the proverbial bee-pasture of husbandry and poetry, the symbol of things cherished and of honeyed and fragrant sweetness.

— Henry Beston, *Herbs and the Earth*

CURRIED LENTILS WITH SAVORY AND THYME

Whether you prefer the inexpensive green lentils or the highly regarded brown French lentils, you'll be rewarded with a dish that's high in protein, calcium, iron, phosphorus, and vitamins A and B-complex. Popular in both European and Middle Eastern cooking, the herbs and spices used here combine the best of both worlds.

Heat the oil in a large pot over medium-high heat. Add the onions and cook, stirring, for about 5 minutes, or until soft. Add the carrots, celery, ginger, and garlic; cook, continuing to stir, for about 5 minutes, or until all are soft and fragrant. Stir in the bay leaf, garam masala or curry, cardamom, thyme, and savory. Reduce heat to medium and cook for 3 minutes.

Add the lentils, vinegar, stock or broth, Worcestershire sauce, and water. Bring to a boil and skim. Reduce heat to low, add salt and pepper, and cover. Cook for 50 minutes to 1 hour, or until lentils are tender. Serve immediately.

Yield: 6 servings

1 tablespoon olive or canola oil
¾ cup chopped yellow onions
½ cup finely chopped carrot
½ cup finely chopped celery
1 tablespoon peeled and minced fresh gingerroot
3 garlic cloves, crushed
1 bay leaf
1 tablespoon garam masala or curry powder
½ teaspoon ground cardamom seeds
Three 4-inch sprigs fresh thyme
Three 4-inch sprigs fresh savory
1 cup brown or green lentils, rinsed well in a strainer
¼ cup white wine vinegar
2 cups vegetable stock or canned vegetable broth
1 teaspoon Worcestershire sauce
1½ cups water
½ teaspoon salt
¼ teaspoon ground black pepper

MALAYSIAN RICE

1 cup jasmine rice
  One 14-ounce can unsweetened
    coconut milk, regular or
    low-fat
½ cup water
  One 1½-inch piece fresh ginger-
    root, peeled and thinly sliced
2 tablespoons thinly sliced
    shallots
1 garlic clove, thinly sliced
½ teaspoon salt
  One 3-inch cinnamon stick
3 whole cloves

In Malaysia this fragrant rice is served for breakfast with hard-boiled eggs, fried peanuts, cucumber slices, and dried anchovies. If granola is more to your early-morning tastes, don't hesitate to try this combination for a light meal or serve as a side dish.

Rinse and drain the rice. Combine rice, coconut milk, water, ginger, shallots, garlic, salt, cinnamon stick, and cloves in a saucepan or electric rice cooker. If using a saucepan, bring to a boil over high heat, then reduce heat to low, cover, and simmer until all liquid is absorbed. If using a rice cooker, follow manufacturer's directions. White jasmine rice will take about 15 minutes to cook; brown jasmine rice, about 20 minutes. After all the liquid is absorbed, check the rice for doneness. If not fully cooked, add a little water and cook for a few more minutes. After the rice is done, let it sit for 5 minutes before serving.
Yield: 4 servings

GREEN RICE

❖

Mounds of rice verdant with herbs: there are few better ways to explore and use herbs in all their glory. Don't limit yourself to any one combination. And try the technique with other rices and grains, including kasha, quinoa, or millet.

Heat the oil in a large saucepan over medium-high heat. Add the onion and cook, stirring, for about 8 minutes, or until soft. Add the bay leaf and rice and cook for 1 minute, stirring. Pour in stock or broth, bring to a boil, and reduce heat to low. Cover and cook for 15 minutes. Stir in the herbs, lemon zest, and pepper. Serve immediately, or refrigerate and serve cold.

Yield: 8 servings

2 tablespoons olive oil
1½ cups chopped yellow onions
1 bay leaf
2 cups long-grain white rice
4 cups vegetable stock or canned vegetable broth
1 cup coarsely chopped fresh herb leaves, such as ½ cup parsley, ⅓ cup dill, and 3 tablespoons tarragon
Minced zest of 1 lemon (about 2 to 3 teaspoons)
½ teaspoon ground black pepper

DHAL WITH VEGETABLES AND HERBS

❖

Whether spelled "dal," "dhal," or "dhall," the term is an Indian word referring either to sixty or more various dried legume seeds or to a spicy dish containing one of these pulses (edible seeds) along with vegetables, herbs, and spices. Usually served with curried dishes, dhal is hearty enough to be a meal in itself.

Rinse and drain the lentils. Combine lentils, water, 1 teaspoon oil, garlic, and ginger in a saucepan and bring to a boil over high heat. Reduce heat to low, cover, and cook until lentils are soft, then stir in potatoes, eggplant, and turmeric. Continue cooking, covered, until potatoes are tender. Set aside.

For less "heat," remove seeds from crushed chile pepper. In a skillet, combine 2 teaspoons oil, crushed chile pepper, mustard seeds, and shallot and cook over medium-high heat, stirring occasionally, until fragrant. Stir into lentil mixture, cover, let sit for 5 minutes, then stir again and serve. The cilantro relish (page 77) is especially good with this.

Yield: 6 servings

Note: *Peeled, seeded tomatoes and/or okra may be added with the potato and eggplant.*

1 cup red, yellow, or brown lentils
2 cups water
1 teaspoon canola oil
2 garlic cloves, minced
1 teaspoon minced fresh gingerroot
1 pound potatoes, cut into ½-inch pieces
1 pound eggplant, cut into ½-inch pieces
½ teaspoon ground turmeric seeds
2 teaspoons canola oil
1 dried red chile pepper, crushed
1 teaspoon brown mustard seeds
1 shallot, thinly sliced

RISOTTO WITH WINTER VEGETABLES AND SAUTÉED MUSHROOMS

❖

6 tablespoons butter
¼ cup chopped yellow onions
2 cups arborio rice
1 cup white wine
3½ cups vegetable stock or canned
      vegetable broth,
      heated to a simmer
2 miniature pumpkins, or 1 small
      winter squash, cut into
      ½-inch cubes
1 small parsnip, peeled and diced
½ pound mushrooms, sliced
½ cup minced fresh parsley leaves
2 tablespoons minced fresh
      thyme leaves
2 tablespoons grated Parmesan
      cheese
½ teaspoon salt
⅛ teaspoon ground black pepper

Although risotto is not a dish for the impatient, the rewards for the diligent merit its preparation. Both parsley and thyme overwinter well indoors or in a cold frame, so there's no excuse not to use fresh herbs, even when winds howl outside.

Melt 2 tablespoons butter in a saucepan over medium heat. Add onions, cover, and cook until soft and translucent. Stir in rice, cover, and cook for 2 minutes. Stir in wine and cook uncovered until liquid is completely absorbed, stirring constantly. Add heated stock or broth 1 cup at a time, waiting between additions until liquid is absorbed, continuing to stir. Reserve remaining ½ cup of broth.

Meanwhile, melt 4 tablespoons butter in a large skillet over medium heat. Stir in parsnip and pumpkin or squash and cook for 20 minutes, or until tender. Remove vegetables. Add mushrooms and the ½ cup of reserved broth to the skillet. Cook until liquid is reduced by half. Stir in parsley and thyme. Stir vegetables, Parmesan cheese, salt, and pepper into the cooked risotto. Serve with mushrooms over the top.
Yield: 6 to 8 servings

GOOD VEGETABLE AND HERB COMBINATIONS

The best way to discover what herbs complement the taste of various vegetables is to experiment. Here are a few combinations to try.
Asparagus. Basil, lemon basil, lemon verbena, lemongrass
Broccoli. Lemongrass, lemon verbena, garlic, ginger
Carrots. Mint, chives, dill
Cauliflower. Rosemary, basil, caraway, dill, tarragon
Corn. Basil, chile pepper
Green beans. Basil, thyme, savory, marjoram
Peas. Marjoram, savory, mint, dill, basil, rosemary
Potatoes. Chives, garlic chives, rosemary, garlic, parsley
Summer squash. Oregano, marjoram, dill, ginger, rosemary, basil, lemon basil, chives, garlic chives

Rosemary-Olive Oatmeal Batter Bread (page 102) ▶

Breads &
Muffins

ROSEMARY-OLIVE OATMEAL BATTER BREAD

2 to 2½ cups unbleached or
   all-purpose flour
¾ cup old-fashioned rolled oats
¼ cup minced fresh rosemary
   leaves
1 teaspoon salt
1 package active dry yeast
1 cup water
¼ cup honey
¼ cup canola oil
1 cup pitted, chopped ripe olives

Batter yeast breads, which don't require kneading, are also a boon to those lacking the luxury of time. Although their texture is more coarse than that of traditional yeast breads, their aroma and flavor still make them a special treat. The combination of rosemary and olives creates a bread ideal for serving with summer vegetables, traditional pastas, or grilled meats, as well as for making sandwiches.

In a large bowl, combine 1 cup flour, oats, rosemary, salt, and yeast, blending well. In a small saucepan, combine water, honey, and oil and heat until hot (120°–130°F). Add liquid to flour mixture. Using an electric mixer, preferably with a dough hook, blend at low speed until moistened. Beat 3 minutes at medium speed. With mixer on low, beat in olives, then the remaining flour in ½-cup increments, until a stiff batter is formed.

Loosely cover the batter with plastic wrap sprayed with nonstick cooking spray. Let rise in a warm (80°–85°F) place about 30 minutes, or until doubled in size.

Spray a 1½-quart baking dish or 8 by 4-inch or 9 by 5-inch loaf pan with nonstick cooking spray. Stir batter, then pour into the prepared baking dish or pan. Cover loosely and let rise in a warm place about 20 minutes, or until batter reaches the top of the container.

During the last rising, heat oven to 375°F. Uncover dough and bake 40 to 45 minutes, or until loaf is golden brown and sounds hollow when lightly tapped. Remove loaf from container and cool on a wire rack.
Yield: 1 loaf

Note: All of the yeast breads can also be made with a 50/50 blend of whole wheat flour and bread flour.

*Unspoiled of April's rain,
by August's fire,
   And incorrupt before
   October's gold,
Green in December's snows
   — such I desire
To be the memory of good
friends of old:
Unchanged, unfearing,
fragrant, as the semblance
   Of Rosemary in my
heart's garden of
remembrance.*

— George P. Baker

LEMON THYME BATTER BREAD

❖

Thyme is one of the most adaptable of herbs, with its ability to enhance a wide range of foods. Lemon thyme offers extra zest. Make chicken or crab salad sandwiches with this bread, or serve toasted with some thyme-flavored herb butter and jelly.

In a small bowl, stir together yeast, water, and 1 teaspoon honey. Let stand for 5 minutes, or until the yeast covers the surface with bubbles. Stir in milk and salt.

In a large bowl, cream the butter, then add the remaining honey and continue to beat until butter is light and fluffy. Beat in eggs, one at a time, or egg substitute, ¼ cup at a time. Stir in lemon thyme and lemon zest.

Alternately add portions of the unbleached or all-purpose and whole wheat flours and yeast mixture, beating well after each addition. Loosely cover the batter with plastic wrap sprayed with nonstick cooking spray. Let rise in a warm (80°–85°F) place about 1 hour, or until doubled in bulk.

Beat the batter 100 strokes by hand or 1 minute with an electric mixer, preferably with a dough hook. Turn into two 9 by 5-inch or 8 by 4-inch loaf pans coated with nonstick cooking spray. Cover and let rise about 30 minutes, or until doubled in size.

During the last rising, heat oven to 350°F. Bake loaves 30 to 40 minutes, or until golden and firm to the touch. Cool briefly in the pan, then turn out on a rack to cool completely.

Yield: 2 loaves

2 packages active dry yeast
⅓ cup very warm (105°–110°F) water
¼ cup honey
1 cup very warm (105°–110°F) milk
½ teaspoon salt
½ cup (1 stick) butter, at room temperature
4 large eggs or 1 cup egg substitute, at room temperature
¼ cup lemon thyme leaves
1 teaspoon grated lemon zest
3 cups unbleached or all-purpose flour
1 cup whole wheat flour

Sybil Kunkel's Sourdough Potato-Wheat Herb Bread

.... ❖ ....

An excellent herb gardener, cook, and friend, Sybil got the starter and recipe for this luscious bread many years ago. Using potatoes is an old-fashioned way to give bread an incredible texture. And don't forget to try other herb combinations! Also remember that the flavor of the bread improves with age.

Potato Sourdough Starter

1 cup very warm (105°–110°F) water
1½ cups sugar
6 tablespoons instant potato flakes
1 package active dry yeast
1 cup hot (120°–130°F) water

Bread

1½ cups very warm (105°–110°F) water
½ cup canola oil
¼ cup sugar
2 teaspoons salt
3 cups bread flour
3 cups whole wheat flour
1 teaspoon minced fresh rosemary leaves
1 teaspoon minced fresh thyme leaves
1 teaspoon minced fresh marjoram leaves
1 teaspoon minced fresh oregano leaves

What I say is that, if a fellow really likes potatoes, he must be a pretty decent fellow.

— A. A. Milne

To make the starter, combine warm water, ¾ cup sugar, 3 tablespoons potato flakes, and yeast in a nonmetallic container. Let sit at room temperature, uncovered, for 8 to 12 hours. Refrigerate, loosely covered, for 7 days. Stir in hot water, ¾ cup sugar, and 3 tablespoons potato flakes. Let sit at room temperature, uncovered, for 12 hours. Totaling 2 cups, the starter is now ready; use 1 cup for making bread and keep the other refrigerated, loosely covered.

The starter must be "fed" each week with 1 cup hot water, ¾ cup sugar, and 3 tablespoons potato flakes, then allowed to rise 12 hours, before using 1 cup again for bread and putting the other cup back in the refrigerator. Even if you don't make bread every week, this procedure must be repeated, either throwing out the cup or giving it to a friend.

To make bread, combine 1 cup of starter with the water, oil, sugar, and salt in a large nonmetallic bowl. Mix well. Stir in the bread and whole wheat flours, 1 cup at a time, thoroughly beating after each addition, until a stiff dough is formed. Put the dough in a large oiled bowl, turning it to oil the surface. Loosely cover dough with a damp cloth or plastic wrap sprayed with nonstick cooking spray. Let rise in a warm (80°–85°F) place for 8 to 12 hours, or until doubled in bulk.

Combine rosemary, thyme, marjoram, and oregano in a small bowl. Punch the dough down and divide into three equal pieces. Roll one piece of dough into a 9 by 6-inch rectangle. Sprinkle the surface evenly with one-third of the herb mixture. Starting at one long side, roll up the dough, tuck under the ends, and place in a 9 by 4-inch or 8 by 4-inch loaf pan that has been lightly coated with nonstick cooking spray. Repeat with the other two pieces of dough. Let rise 4 to 8 hours in a warm place, or until doubled in bulk.

Heat oven to 350°F and bake loaves for 25 to 35 minutes, or until golden brown. Remove loaves from the pans and cool on a rack. For a soft crust, brush the tops of loaves with canola oil or melted butter after removing from the oven.
Yield: 3 loaves

Marjoram

MARJORAMS ARE NATIVE
to a wide area extending
from Europe to
northern Africa and
southwestern Asia.
They have been
prized since the
time of the ancient
Egyptians and
Greeks. At first
marjorams were mainly
used medicinally, playing a role in
massage oils and baths for healing
aches and pains and preventing
baldness. Taken internally, marjoram was used to aid the stomach,
sore throats, and congestion.

For cooking, look for plants
labeled sweet marjoram, *Origanum
majorana*, or *O.* x *majoricum*.

Small amounts of fresh marjoram
can be harvested whenever needed.
To obtain the greatest yield for drying, pinch out the flower buds when
they appear, then harvest when the
flower buds appear again, cutting
off to about 2 inches high.

FEARRINGTON HOUSE PROVENCAL PICNIC BASKET BREAD

❖

One 12-ounce can or bottle of beer
1 cup very warm (105°–110°F) water
1 package active dry yeast
6 cups unbleached or all-purpose flour
1 teaspoon salt
2 tablespoons dry herbes de Provence (see opposite page or purchase at a specialty food store)
3 ounces country ham, minced
1 large egg yolk, at room temperature
2 teaspoons water

Jenny Fitch, proprietor of an elegant restaurant, bed-and-breakfast, and shopping complex in Chapel Hill, North Carolina, includes this distinctively shaped bread in The Fearrington House Cookbook. *Utilizing a dried herb mixture known as herbes de Provence, it indeed bespeaks sunny climes and an alfresco meal. But then, it would make even a gray, chilly day bright.*

Warm the beer by running hot water over the can or bottle for a few minutes. In a large bowl, combine the beer, water, and yeast. Let sit for a few minutes until the yeast bubbles. Add 3 cups flour and mix thoroughly with a spoon or electric mixer.

Cover with a piece of plastic wrap coated with nonstick cooking spray. Put in a warm (80°–85°F) place for about 8 hours, or until the mixture rises and falls down.

Add the remaining 3 cups flour and the salt. Mix thoroughly by hand or electric mixer and turn out onto a lightly floured surface. Use a pastry scraper to keep turning the mixture until it clings together and becomes possible to knead. Pat into a circle and add the herb mixture and country ham. Fold the mixture in half and knead for another 10 to 12 minutes.

Using three-fourths of the dough, shape half of it into a round ball and put it in the bottom of a charlotte mold (7 inches in diameter and 4 inches deep) coated with nonstick cooking spray. Cut the remaining portion into four sections.

On an unfloured surface, roll two sections into 12-inch ropes. Twist them together and place across the middle of the dough in the charlotte mold, tucking the ends under. Repeat with the other two sections, placing the second twist perpendicular to the first. Use the remaining dough to make a baguette.

Heat oven to 375°F. Loosely cover the loaves and let them rise about 40 minutes, or until doubled in bulk. Brush with an egg yolk glaze made by whisking the yolk with water. Bake for 25 minutes, then reduce heat to 350°F and bake for an additional 35 minutes, or until golden and hollow-sounding when tapped. The baguette should be done in about 35 minutes.

Yield: One 7-inch loaf and 1 baguette

Note: A 2½-quart metal mixing bowl can be substituted for the charlotte mold.

CHICKPEA FLATBREAD WITH GARLIC CHIVES, CILANTRO, AND GINGER

Serve this traditional herb-rich Indian bread with either a salad or main course or with plain yogurt as a snack. Garlic chives, also known as Chinese chives, are widely used in Asian cooking. Among the easiest of herbs to grow, they are also very hardy and stays green for much of the year, especially if grown in a cold frame.

- **1 cup chickpea flour (available at Indian or Middle Eastern groceries)**
- **1 teaspoon whole cumin seeds**
- **1 teaspoon salt**
- **¼ teaspoon ground hot red pepper**
- **¾ cup water**
- **½ cup minced fresh garlic chives**
- **¼ cup minced fresh cilantro leaves**
- **1 teaspoon minced fresh gingerroot**
- **½ cup peeled, seeded, and diced tomatoes**

Cilantro

In a large bowl, combine flour, cumin seeds, salt, and red pepper. Add the water and mix well. Stir in the garlic chives, cilantro, ginger, and tomato. The batter should be slightly thicker than pancake batter. If too thin, add a bit more flour and mix well.

Coat a large nonstick skillet or griddle with nonstick cooking spray and place over medium-high heat. For each flatbread, put 2 tablespoons of batter in the pan and spread it out with the back of a spoon until uniformly thick and about 4 inches in diameter. Cook for 1 minute, then turn over and cook for 2 minutes on the other side. If necessary, turn over again to finish cooking. Dark spots mean the bread is sufficiently cooked. Serve immediately.
Yield: 8 to 10 flatbreads

HERBES DE PROVENCE

This heady blend of Mediterranean herbs may contain as few as five or as many as eleven different herbs, both pungent and sweet. Thyme is the dominant herb, but rosemary, savory, fennel seeds, marjoram, and lavender flowers are just as important. Other possibilities are sage, basil, mint, oregano, and bay. During the growing season the blend may be made from fresh herbs instead of dried. Although herbes de Provence can be bought in specialty foodstores or by mail-order, a homemade blend is easy to make.

Dry the herbs separately, then combine in the following proportions: 4 parts thyme leaves, 2 parts rosemary leaves, 2 parts basil leaves, 2 parts savory leaves, 2 parts marjoram leaves, 1 part lavender flowers, and 1 part fennel seeds. Store in an airtight container.

FOCACCIA WITH FRESH HERBS

❖

½ teaspoon active dry yeast
½ teaspoon sugar
¾ cup very warm (105°–110°F)
   water
2¾ cups unbleached or
   all-purpose flour
½ teaspoon salt
¼ cup extra-virgin olive oil
2 tablespoons fresh herb leaves
½ teaspoon kosher, or coarse, salt

Adapted from Elizabeth Romer's Italian Pizza and Hearth Breads, *this pizza-like flatbread flavored with herbs and olive oil is usually served with a meal. For the most authentic results, bake the bread on a baking stone and use herbs associated with Italian cuisine, such as oregano, basil, rosemary, or marjoram — in any combination that pleases you.*

Sprinkle the yeast and sugar into ½ cup very warm water. Let stand about 10 minutes, or until the surface becomes bubbly. In a large bowl, combine the flour and salt. Make a well in the center. Pour in the yeast mixture and 1 tablespoon olive oil. Stir well with a wooden spoon or electric mixer. Continuing to stir, slowly add ¼ cup very warm water. The dough will be soft and slightly sticky.

Turn the dough out onto a very lightly floured surface. Knead for 10 minutes, adding a small spoonful of flour only if absolutely necessary. Put the dough in a warm (80°–85°F) place, loosely cover with plastic wrap sprayed with nonstick cooking spray or a damp cloth, and let rise until doubled in bulk, or about 1 hour.

Turn the dough out onto a lightly floured surface and knead gently several times, then flatten out to a 10-inch circle. Place it on an oiled baking stone, pizza pan, or heavy cookie sheet. Press indentations with your fingers to give it dimples. Loosely cover and let rise in a warm place about 45 minutes, or until doubled in bulk.

Heat oven to 425°F. Combine 3 tablespoons olive oil and herbs in a food processor, blender, or mortar and pestle until the leaves are broken up and the oil is fragrant. Pour herb-oil mixture over the focaccia and rub gently into the surface. Sprinkle the top with salt. Bake 15 minutes, then reduce heat to 400°F and bake 5 minutes more, or until golden brown. Let cool and cut into wedges.
Yield: One 10-inch bread

Oregano

THE NAME OREGANO is derived from the Greek words for "joy of the mountain." The ancient Greeks and Romans crowned wedding couples with oregano, as it was said to banish sadness.

Sorting through the botany of the marjorams and closely related oreganos is the bane of botanists, not to mention gardeners and cooks. There are a number of species and varieties within the genus *Origanum*, and they hybridize readily in nature. Moreover, there are at least fourteen other plants with the flavor of oregano, including *Coleus amboinicus* and *Lippia graveolens*.

Two varieties of oregano are beautiful ornamental plants but have little or no flavor. Golden oregano (*O. vulgare* 'Aureum') has yellow-green leaves on rounded 6- to 12-inch plants. Dittany of Crete (*O. dictamnus*) has round, fuzzy, gray-green leaves and pink hop-like flowers on sprawling stems that are ideal for draping over the edges of pots and windowboxes.

Although oregano may be used anytime, its flavor is best just before flowering. If allowed to flower, the stems should be cut back afterward to rejuvenate growth. Dry oregano for winter use.

HERB-RICOTTA TOMATO QUICK BREAD

❖

2 cups unbleached or
    all-purpose flour
1 tablespoon sugar
1 teaspoon baking powder
½ teaspoon baking soda
¼ teaspoon ground black pepper
1 cup tomato juice
1 cup low-fat or nonfat ricotta
    cheese
2 large eggs, or ½ cup fat-free
    egg substitute
½ cup oil-marinated sun-dried
    tomatoes, drained and minced
¼ cup canola oil
¼ cup minced fresh herbs, such
    as basil, rosemary, thyme,
    marjoram, oregano, chives,
    or lovage

Breads leavened with baking powder and/or baking soda instead of yeast require no rising time and go from start to finish in less than an hour. Using tomato juice, sun-dried tomatoes, ricotta, and Mediterranean herbs gives this bread a strong Italian accent. Serve it with salads, egg dishes, or poached fish, or as a sandwich bread for a twist on the BLT theme.

Heat oven to 350°F. Coat a 9 by 5-inch or 8 by 4-inch loaf pan with nonstick cooking spray and lightly dust with flour. Sift flour, sugar, baking powder, baking soda, salt, and pepper into a large bowl.

In a medium bowl, combine tomato juice, cheese, eggs or egg substitute, tomatoes, oil, and herbs; mix thoroughly. Add liquid mixture to flour mixture, stirring just until dry ingredients are moistened. Pour the batter into the prepared pan. Bake for 50 to 60 minutes, or until a toothpick inserted in the center comes out clean. Cool on a wire rack, then remove from the pan.
Yield: 1 loaf

DRIED TOMATOES MARINATED IN OIL AND HERBS

6 pounds oblong paste tomatoes
    Sprigs of basil
    Head of garlic
    Olive oil

The concentrated flavor of dried tomatoes benefits breads, pizzas, focaccias, salads, and pasta sauces. They are easily made at home in an oven or dehydrator from tomatoes at their peak flavor.

If using a dehydrator, cut tomatoes in half lengthwise and place them skin side down on trays set 2 to 3 inches apart. Dry them on high for 10 to 16 hours, removing smaller tomatoes as they dry.

For oven drying, heat oven to 150°F, or the lowest possible temperature. Cut tomatoes in half lengthwise. Place cut side up on a wire rack. Leave a little space around the tomatoes for air to circulate. Sprinkle lightly with salt. Put in the oven and leave the door slightly ajar for moisture to escape. Rotate racks from front to back and top to bottom every hour or so. Tomatoes are done in 4 to 6 hours, or when they are slightly shriveled and dry but not crisp. Remove as they dry.

Cool and pack into sterilized jars. Layer tomatoes with several leaves or a sprig of basil or other herbs and 1 or 2 peeled garlic cloves to each jar. Add olive oil to cover completely. Securely attach a lid, and store in the refrigerator.
Yield: 2 to 3 pints

CRANBERRY-NUT BREAD WITH GINGER AND FENNEL

❖

The delicate whisper of spice from the fennel is empowered with the anisette liqueur in this quick sweet bread.

Heat oven to 350°F. Coat an 8 by 4-inch or 9 by 5-inch loaf pan with nonstick cooking spray and lightly dust with flour. Sift flour, baking powder, baking soda, and salt into a medium bowl. In a large bowl, cream the sugar, oil, and egg or egg substitute. Alternately add portions of the flour mixture, orange juice, and liqueur or Pernod to the creamed mixture, beating well after each addition. Stir in the cranberries, pecans, fennel, and ginger.

Pour the batter into the prepared pan and bake for 45 minutes, or until a toothpick inserted in the center comes out clean. Cool on a wire rack, then remove from the pan.
Yield: 1 loaf

1 cup boiling water
1 cup dried cranberries
2 cups unbleached or
   all-purpose flour
2 teaspoons baking powder
¼ teaspoon baking soda
½ teaspoon salt
½ cup sugar
2 tablespoons canola oil
1 large egg, or ¼ cup fat-free
   egg substitute
¼ cup orange juice
¼ cup anisette liqueur or Pernod
1 cup cranberries
½ cup chopped pecans
¼ cup chopped fresh fennel leaves
1 teaspoon minced fresh
   gingerroot

CORNBREAD WITH PEACHES AND CINNAMON BASIL

❖

Golden and sweet with the spiciness of cinnamon basil, this bread is an excellent breakfast, afternoon tea, or snack bread. Gild the lily by serving it with homemade peach preserves also flavored with cinnamon basil.

Heat oven to 375°F. Coat an 8 by 8-inch baking pan with nonstick cooking spray and lightly dust with flour. Sift flour, cornmeal, sugar, baking powder, baking soda, and salt into a large bowl. In another bowl, combine the milk, peaches, eggs or egg substitute, butter, and basil. Pour the milk mixture into the flour mixture, stirring just until the dry ingredients are moistened. Do not overmix.

Pour the batter into the prepared pan and bake for 35 minutes, or until the top springs back when lightly touched. Cool on a wire rack, then remove from the pan.
Yield: 6 to 9 servings

1 cup unbleached or
   all-purpose flour
¾ cup yellow cornmeal
¼ cup sugar
½ tablespoon baking powder
½ teaspoon baking soda
¼ teaspoon salt
1 cup milk
½ pound peaches, peeled, pitted,
   and chopped
1 egg, lightly beaten, or ¼ cup
   fat-free egg substitute
2 tablespoons butter, melted
¼ cup minced fresh cinnamon
   basil leaves

TRIPLE ALLIUM MUFFINS

❖

½ cup finely chopped shallots,
 onions, or leeks
¼ cup canola oil
2 cups unbleached or all-purpose
 flour
1 tablespoon sugar
2 teaspoons baking powder
½ teaspoon salt
¼ teaspoon baking soda
1 cup buttermilk
1 large egg, lightly beaten, or
 ¼ cup egg subsitute
¼ cup minced fresh chives
¼ cup minced fresh garlic chives

Savory muffins, aromatic with members of the onion, or allium, clan, most pleasantly accompany a brunch of eggs and fried potatoes or a meal of hearty stew. Both chives and garlic chives are easy to grow almost year-round, either indoors or out. Try different onions, including red, white, yellow, or sweet varieties as well as shallots or leeks.

Heat oven to 375°F. Coat 12 standard-size (2½-inch) muffin cups with nonstick cooking spray and dust lightly with flour.

Heat 1 teaspoon oil in a small skillet over medium heat and cook the shallots, onions, or leeks for 3 minutes, or until soft.

Sift the flour, sugar, baking powder, salt, and baking soda into a large bowl. In a small bowl, combine the cooked onions, remaining oil, buttermilk, egg or egg substitute, chives, and garlic chives; mix well. Pour the onion mixture into the flour mixture, stirring just until the dry ingredients are moistened. Do not overmix.

Fill prepared muffin cups about three-quarters full. Bake for 15 to 20 minutes, or until a toothpick inserted in the center comes out clean. Cool on a wire rack, then remove from the pan.
Yield: Twelve 2½-inch muffins

HERB FLOUR

Breads, muffins, biscuits, scones, cakes, cookies — anything calling for flour will be even better when made with an herb flour. Layer dried herb leaves with flour, leaving for several weeks. Remove the herbs and store the flour in an airtight container. Use a single herb or a mixture, sweet herbs or pungent.

Chives are nice in salad
To cheese, they give a zest,
Are very good in scrambled
 eggs
But I think I like them best
Growing as fringe in the
 garden
A trimming for flower beds
Like rows of little rushes
With dusty pinkish heads.

— L. Young Correthers, *These Blooming Herbs*

BLUEBERRY-SAGE MUFFINS

❖

Very crumbly but with an incredible flavor from the blueberries and sage,
these muffins have a tendency to stick — so be sure to use paper muffin cups
or a nonstick muffin pan with nonstick cooking spray.

2 cups blueberries
2 tablespoons minced fresh sage leaves
½ cup sugar
Minced zest of 1 lemon (2 to 3 teaspoons)
1½ cups unbleached or all-purpose flour
2 teaspoons baking powder
½ teaspoon baking soda
¼ teaspoon salt
1 large egg, or ¼ cup egg substitute
½ cup plain nonfat yogurt or nonfat sour cream
¼ cup milk
2 tablespoons canola oil
1 tablespoon lemon juice

TOPPING

1 tablespoon sugar
½ teaspoon ground cinnamon

In a large bowl, combine the blueberries, sage, sugar, and
lemon zest. Let sit for 30 minutes. Heat oven to 375°F. Line
12 standard-size (2½-inch) muffin cups with paper liners.

Sift flour, baking powder, baking soda, and salt into a large bowl.
To the blueberry mixture, add the egg or egg substitutes or sour
cream, yogurt, milk, oil, and lemon juice. Pour the blueberry mixture
into the flour mixture, stirring just until the dry ingredients are moistened. Do not overmix.

Fill each muffin cup to within ½ inch of the top. Combine sugar
and cinnamon for the topping and sprinkle some on each muffin.
Bake for 25 minutes, or until muffin tops spring back when lightly
touched. Remove from muffin pan and cool on a wire rack.
Yield: Twelve 2½-inch muffins

Sage

SAGE AIDS
DIGESTION.
Sage tea has
been used as a
tonic and cure for
colds and sore throats.
An English version of a
spring tonic involves eating sandwiches made from bread, butter,
and sage leaves as exemplified in
the old saying, "He who would
live for aye must eat sage in May."
Sage is also a traditional component
in herbal shampoos and rinses,
especially for dark hair.

In the seventeenth century, the
Chinese valued sage so much that
they were willing to trade the
Dutch three to four chests of
China tea leaves for one chest of
sage leaves.

A marvelous addition to grape
jam, sage is also good for flavoring honey. Sage honey and jams
make scrumptious bastes for meats
and poultry and offer a unique
flavor change when served with
various breads.

HERB-CHEESE DROP BISCUITS

⧫

1 cup unbleached or
    all-purpose flour
¾ cup whole wheat flour
2 teaspoons baking powder
½ teaspoon salt
⅛ teaspoon ground black pepper
¾ cup shredded summer squash
⅔ cup milk
⅓ cup regular or low-fat cream
    cheese, homemade yogurt
    cheese, or goat cheese, at
    room temperature
1 large egg, lightly beaten, or
    ¼ cup egg substitute
2 tablespoons minced fresh herbs

No rolling pin is needed for these quickly and easily made biscuits flavored with herbs, fresh cheese, and summer squash. Make them with whatever herbs are available, or use herbs that match the rest of the meal. If you want a sweet biscuit, eliminate the black pepper and add 1 teaspoon sugar.

Heat oven to 400°F. Lightly spray a baking sheet with nonstick cooking spray or cover with parchment.

Sift flours, baking powder, salt, and pepper into a medium bowl. In a small bowl, combine squash, milk, cheese, egg or egg substitute, and herbs; mix well. Add liquid mixture to flour mixture, stirring just until dry ingredients are moistened. Do not overmix.

Drop ¼ cup of dough onto baking sheet for each biscuit, spacing 2 inches apart. Bake 15 to 20 minutes, or until golden brown. Serve immediately.
Yield: 12 biscuits

APPLE–LEMON VERBENA COMPOTE

2 tablespoons butter
2 pounds cooking apples,
    peeled, cored, and cut into
    ¾-inch dice
2 whole cloves
¼ teaspoon ground allspice
1 tablespoon sugar
1 bay leaf
½ cup fresh lemon verbena leaves
¼ cup plus ¾ cup apple juice
¼ cup lemon juice

In a large saucepan, melt the butter over medium-high heat until it foams, then add the apples, cloves, allspice, sugar, and bay leaf. Stirring, cook until almost dry. Stir in the lemon verbena and ¼ cup apple juice. (Meanwhile, mix the ¾ cup apple juice and ¼ cup lemon juice together in a measuring cup.) Reduce heat to low, cover, and cook for 40 minutes, adding a tablespoon of the apple-lemon juice mixture to the compote every 10 minutes, or as needed to keep it from drying out. The compote is done when its color is light brown and the apples are halfway broken down. Serve warm or chilled.
Yield: 2 cups

LEMONY SCONES

❖

For breakfast in bed, brunch, or afternoon tea, these tender, sweet scones with the subtle tang of citrus from lemon verbena leaves have a special delicacy that always charms. Serve with Apple–Lemon Verbena Compote (see previous page).

Sift the all-purpose and cake flours, sugar, baking powder, baking soda, and salt into a large mixing bowl. With a pastry cutter or an electric mixer, cut in the butter a piece at a time. The mixture should resemble small loose pebbles. Quickly stir in the raisins, currants, and lemon verbena. Pour in the buttermilk and beat for 5 to 10 seconds, or until the mixture climbs the sides of the bowl. Do not overmix. Put the dough onto a piece of plastic wrap, close tightly, and refrigerate for 1 hour.

Heat oven to 400°F. Turn the chilled dough out onto a lightly floured surface and roll to 1-inch thick. Cut out scones with a 2-inch round or fluted cutter and space 2 inches apart on a parchment covered baking sheet. Bake for 12 to 15 minutes, or until golden. Serve immediately.

Yield: Twelve 2-inch scones

1 cup unbleached or all-purpose flour
⅓ cup sugar
1 cup plus 2 tablespoons cake flour
1 tablespoon baking powder
1 teaspoon baking soda
¼ teaspoon salt
6 tablespoons butter, very cold and cut into ½-inch pieces
½ cup golden raisins
¼ cup dried currants
3 tablespoons finely chopped fresh lemon verbena leaves
⅔ cup buttermilk

HERB PUFF PASTRY TWISTS

.... ❖ ....

Quick and easy to make, these airy breadsticks are flavored with herbs and butter. Serve them with appetizers, soups, salads, or main courses. Best of all, here's a chance to either choose your favorite herbs or match herbs with other foods — for example, basil with tomato soup or sage with a grilled chicken salad.

1 package frozen puff pastry
¼ cup (½ stick) unsalted butter, melted

Heat oven to 400°F. Thaw pastry for 20 minutes. Combine the butter and herbs. On a lightly floured board, cut the pastry into strips ¾ inch wide and 10 inches long.

Brush the strips with the butter-herb mixture. Twist each strip three or four times and lay on an ungreased baking sheet. Bake for 8 to 10 minutes, or until golden brown. Let cool slightly, then serve immediately.

Yield: 24 pieces

HERB BUTTERS

Herb butters may have lost some of their cachet as a result of the concern over dietary fats, but they're a perfect opportunity to practice your moderation. Nothing is more resplendent with simply cooked vegetables and baked potatoes, as well as breads, muffins, biscuits, or grilled meats.

Use just one herb or a mixture, in the proportion of 1 tablespoon minced herbs to 4 tablespoons (½ stick) butter at room temperature. Mix in the herbs thoroughly, then add 1 teaspoon lemon juice. Store in an airtight container in the refrigerator. Or, shape into logs or balls or use a butter mold, cover tightly and refrigerate. The butter may also be frozen. Small covered condiment cups, available from restaurant suppliers, are useful for storing serving-sized portions of flavored butters.

Which herbs to use in making butters? Experiment with them all, even with herb seeds and edible flowers.

Harvesting Fresh Herbs

THE BEST TIME TO PICK HERBS is on a cool, dry morning, but don't hesitate to gather herbs anytime they're needed.

The essential oils in the leaves of herbs are at their peak just before the herbs bloom, but that doesn't mean they aren't flavorful at other times. This is just the best time to harvest for preserving.

To harvest herb seeds such as anise, caraway, dill, fennel, or lovage, wait until they turn brown but before they open. Snip the heads into a paper bag. Put in a warm, dark place until the seeds have fallen, then store in a tightly closed jar — preferably in the refrigerator to prevent weevils. You can also prevent weevils by dipping whole seed heads in boiling water, then drying and proceeding as before.

The simplest way to freeze herbs is to blanch them, dip briefly in ice water, drain, pat dry, and spread them out on baking sheets to freeze. Once frozen, store in airtight bags or containers. Another way is to purée the herbs with a small amount of water and freeze as ice cubes, storing the cubes in airtight plastic bags.

Peach and Lavender Tart (page 118) ▶

Desserts

PEACH AND LAVENDER TART

· ❖ ·

**One 9-inch pastry shell,
store-bought or homemade**
**2 pounds peaches, split, pitted,
and cut in ¼-inch slices**
3 tablespoons lemon juice
⅓ cup sugar
**1 tablespoon lavender flowers,
gently crushed**
⅔ cup blanched almonds
**1 large egg, or ¼ cup fat-free
egg substitute**
2 tablespoons butter

*Peaches and lavender — two of the most beloved flavors and scents. Add a
layer of almonds (a relative of peaches) and the result is unsurpassable!*

Heat oven to 350°F. Line the pastry shell with parchment paper
and put in at least ½ inch of pie weights or dry beans. Bake the
shell for 15 minutes, then remove the parchment and weights,
reduce heat to 325°F, and bake for 8 minutes or just until the bottom
is dry. Set aside to cool.

In a large bowl, combine peaches, lemon juice, 2 tablespoons sugar,
and lavender. Toss and let stand for at least 1 hour.

Put the almonds in a small baking dish and toast in the oven for
about 8 minutes, or until golden. Break up the almonds in a food
processor, then add the remaining sugar, egg or egg substitute, and
butter; process until blended but chunky. Spread the almond mixture
over the bottom of the pastry shell.

When the peaches have given up about ¼ cup of juice, drain them
well, reserving the juice. Spread half the peaches over the almond
mix, then arrange the remaining half in a spiral pattern on top.

Bake the tart at 325°F for 50 minutes, lightly brushing the top with
the reserved juice three times during the baking. To keep the crust
from becoming too brown, cover the rim with aluminum foil until the
last 15 minutes of baking. Cool and serve.
Yield: 6 to 8 servings

*All the seasons run
   their race
In this quiet resting place;
Peach and apricot and fig
Here will ripen
   and grow big.*

— Henry Austin Dobson

LEMON VERBENA CRÈME BRÛLÉE

❖

*The delicate essence of lemon intrigues in this sophisticated baked custard
with a broiled brown sugar crust. Blanching the lemon verbena leaves
removes any excess water that might seep out into the cream as it cooks.*

¼ **cup fresh lemon verbena leaves**
4 **large egg yolks**
¼ **cup sugar**
2 **cups heavy cream**
1 **vanilla bean**
¼ **cup light brown sugar, sifted or sieved**

Heat oven to 275°F. Bring a small saucepan of water to a boil over
high heat and plunge the lemon verbena leaves into the water for
20 seconds. Immediately plunge them into ice water. Drain and
press dry between paper towels. Set aside.

Whip the egg yolks and sugar in a mixer or with a whisk, until they
lighten in color and the sugar dissolves. The mixture should form a
"ribbon" coming off the beaters or whisk.

Combine the cream and vanilla bean in a small saucepan and bring
just to a simmer over low heat. Remove from the heat, skim off any
foam, and remove the vanilla bean. Slowly pour the cream into the
egg-sugar mixture, beating constantly.

Distribute the lemon verbena leaves among six 6-ounce custard
ramekins. Pour the cream mixture over the leaves. Put the ramekins
in a baking pan filled with 1 inch of boiling water. Bake for 45 minutes, or until the edges are set and the center is still loose. Cool,
cover, and refrigerate. If leaves rise to the top, gently peel them off
and discard.

Just before serving, heat the oven broiler. Sprinkle the brown
sugar in an even layer over the tops of the baked custards and put
them on a baking sheet. Place under the broiler. Watch carefully;
when the sugar is melted and shiny, remove them immediately. Let
sit for 2 minutes, then serve.

Variation: Substitute 6 fresh or dried bay leaves for the lemon verbena.
Yield: 6 servings

Lemon Verbena

LEMON VERBENA is one
of the few
popular herbs
that is native
to South America,
where it grows naturally
in Argentina, Chile,
and Peru.

Retaining its
intense lemon flavor when cooked,
lemon verbena is the premier
"lemon herb" for seasoning salad
dressings, marinades, drinks, breads,
grains, vegetables, fish, poultry, butters, jellies, vinegars, and desserts.
Use it either fresh or dried.

Fresh lemon verbena leaves are
somewhat tough, so they are usually
either finely minced or used whole
and removed before serving.

A component of commercial
colognes, toilet waters, bath oils,
and soaps, lemon verbena is enjoyed
in homemade ways by adding it to
baths, finger bowls, potpourris,
bouquets, and tussy-mussies.
Lemon verbena tea helps to settle
an upset stomach.

FRESH FIGS WITH MASCARPONE AND FENNEL

❖

1 cup mascarpone cheese
2 tablespoons sugar
1½ tablespoons lemon juice
⅓ cup minced fresh fennel leaves
12 fresh figs

The incredible richness of the Italian cream cheese paired with the melting ambrosia of fresh figs becomes a triumvirate simple yet sublime with the addition of the delicately spicy taste of fennel.

Mix the mascarpone cheese, sugar, lemon juice, and fennel in a small bowl. Cover and let stand for 1 hour to allow the flavor to develop.

To prepare each fig, cut off the stem, then cut in quarters from top to just short of the bottom. Pull back the quarters to open a space large enough for stuffing. Fill each fig with a heaping tablespoon of cheese mixture. Serve immediately.
Yield: 4 to 6 servings

GRAPEFRUIT AND ROSEMARY SORBET

❖

2 tablespoons minced
    grapefruit zest
    Two 5-inch sprigs fresh
    rosemary
3 cups grapefruit juice
⅓ cup sugar
3 tablespoons light corn syrup

Whether used as a palate-cleansing refreshment between courses of a meal or as a light dessert for a simple supper, the combination of grapefruit juice and rosemary yields a tantalizing treat. Be sure to use the best quality fresh-squeezed grapefruit juice. Experiment with pink grapefruit juice, too.

Combine 1 tablespoon grapefruit zest, the rosemary, 1 cup juice, and the sugar in a small saucepan. Cook over low heat until the sugar has dissolved, or about 10 minutes. Do not allow the mixture to boil.

Cool, remove rosemary, and add the remaining 2 tablespoons zest and 2 cups juice. Stir in the corn syrup. Pour the mixture into an ice-cream freezer and freeze according to the manufacturer's directions.
Yield: 1 quart

HONEYED MELON AND GRAPES WITH MINT

*This is your chance to experiment with some of the more exotic mints —
pineapple, orange, grapefruit, apple, even chocolate! Of course, "regular"
spearmint or peppermint will do quite nicely, too. No matter which you
choose, the result is refreshing, beautiful, and healthful.*

 2 cups melon balls (use cantaloupe, honeydew, or other melons
    alone or in a mixture)
 2 cups red seedless grapes, cut in half
 2 tablespoons honey
 1 tablespoon lemon juice
 ¼ cup mint leaves, gently crushed

Combine the melon, grapes, honey, lemon juice, and mint leaves in
a large bowl. Let stand for 1 hour, tossing occasionally, to allow
the flavors to blend. Serve at room temperature or chilled.
Yield: 6 servings

HERB HONEY

Honey gathered from the nectar of herb flowers may be renowned, but few of us are
apt to have the inclination for raising bees. A more than adequate substitute is to
flavor a mild honey with herbs and flowers. Stir together 3 parts honey to 1 part
fresh herbs, making sure the leaves are totally submerged. Steep in a tightly closed
jar for 1 to 3 weeks, or until the desired flavor is reached. Strain out the herbs and store.

Some favored herbs to use for flavoring honey include thyme, rosemary, lavender,
and rose geranium. Of course, herb honeys can be used in cooking, but don't forget
to keep some readily available for spooning into a cup of tea or whipping with butter
for spreading on breads.

*If whiffs of all the Fragrant
  Herbs
Could have a special tint,
How lovely would the color be
Above a bed of Mint.*

— Marguerite H. Hickernel and Ella W. Brewer,
Adam's Herbs

COLD LEMON MOUSSE WITH CASSIS AND VIOLAS

❖

2 large eggs plus 2 large egg
    yolks, lightly beaten together
9 tablespoons lemon juice
    Minced zest of 1 lemon
    (about 2 to 3 teaspoons)
½ cup plus 1 tablespoon sugar
½ cup (1 stick) butter, very cold,
    cut into ½-inch pieces
1 cup crème de cassis
1 cup crème fraîche (see box)
1 cup heavy cream
3 to 4 dozen fresh viola flowers

A joyful little circlet of violas crowns this ephemeral dessert of lemon and black currant layers. To encourage the enchantment, use a tiny bit of the cassis liqueur in champagne to make a kir royale as an accompaniment.

Combine the eggs and egg yolks, lemon juice, lemon zest, and ½ cup sugar in a small saucepan. Cook over low heat, stirring constantly, until mixture is just hot. Add the butter, bit by bit, stirring and scraping the bottom and sides. Cook until the mixture begins to thicken and coats the spoon like custard. Cool and refrigerate.

Combine the cassis and 1 tablespoon sugar in a small saucepan over medium heat and cook until reduced by half. The mixture will be slightly syrupy. Pour into a small bowl and cool to room temperature. Fold in the crème fraîche and refrigerate.

In a small chilled bowl, use chilled beaters to whip the heavy cream to stiff peaks. Fold the whipped cream into the chilled lemon mixture. To serve, put a layer of the lemon mousse in a wine, champagne, or parfait glass, then add a layer of the cassis cream. Top with a dollop of lemon mousse or plain whipped cream and an arrangement of violas.

Yield: 6 servings

CRÈME FRAÎCHE

To make a reasonable facsimile of crème fraîche at home, whisk 2 tablespoons of sour cream or buttermilk into 1 cup heavy cream until completely smooth. Leave uncovered or cover with cheesecloth at room temperature for 8 to 12 hours. When thick and hard to pour, cover tightly and refrigerate.

We are closer to the vegetable kingdom than we know; it is not for us alone that mint, thyme, sage, and rosemary exhale "brush me and eat me!" — for us that . . . coffeeberry, tea-plant and vine perfect themselves. Their aim is to be absorbed by man, although they can achieve it only attaching themselves to roast mutton.

— Cyril Connolly, *The Unquiet Grave*

Viola

LEGEND HAS IT that Zeus's paramour, Io, was discovered by his wife Hera, who, in a jealous rage, turned Io into a white heifer. Where Io's tears fell, violets sprung forth. Throughout history, lore, and literature, violets have been associated with modesty, innocence, and love.

Violets were a favorite of Napoleon and became a French political symbol when he was banished to Elba. Before leaving, his words reportedly were, "I will return with the violets in spring!" Indeed, he did return in March 1815, and the streets were strewn with violets. Napoleon marked each anniversary with Josephine with a bouquet of violets. When he died, his locket was found to contain pressed violets from Josephine's grave.

Violets *(Viola odorata)* are extremely high in vitamin C. Crystallized flowers make a lovely garnish for cakes, cookies, or ice cream. Violet syrup adds a delicate flavor to sponge or angel cakes. Use fresh flowers to adorn fruit cups and salads. Using distilled water, freeze violet blooms in ice cube trays for a lovely addition to summer drinks. Violet leaves may be added to salads or tea sandwiches.

Johnny-jump-ups and pansies can be used as edible flowers.

Bread Pudding with Lemon Verbena and Fresh Berry Sauce

························· ❖ ·························

Bread Pudding

Twelve ½-inch slices bread, crusts removed
3 cups milk
1 cup minced fresh lemon verbena leaves
½ teaspoon pure vanilla extract
¼ teaspoon salt
⅛ teaspoon grated nutmeg
3 large eggs, lightly beaten, or ¾ cup fat-free egg substitute
⅓ cup sugar
1 teaspoon lemon juice

Berry Sauce

2 tablespoons butter
4 cups strawberries, hulled and cut in half
3 tablespoons sugar
1 tablespoon lemon juice
2 cups red raspberries

Pots filled with lemon verbena standing on the terrace of the porch where we drink tea or after-dinner coffee give off their pleasant perfume as we walk past them and our clothes or hands touch their leaves.

— Helen Morgenthau Fox, *Gardening with Herbs*

For a homespun dessert that originated as a use for stale bread, this baked custard-and-bread mélange is now found on some rather impressive menus. Use bread with a good, sturdy texture, such as Italian or French, either homemade or from a bakery. Besides white, try challah, brioche, raisin, spelt, or wheat bread.

To make the bread pudding, heat oven to 250°F. Place the bread slices in a single layer on baking sheets and toast about 15 minutes, or until thoroughly dried out. Increase oven temperature to 300°F.

In a large bowl, combine the milk, lemon verbena, vanilla, salt, and nutmeg. Tear the toasted bread into pieces and stir into the liquid. Let sit about 10 minutes, or until the liquid is absorbed.

In a small bowl, combine the eggs or egg substitute, sugar, and lemon juice. Beat until the mixture turns light yellow and a ribbon forms when the beaters are lifted. Stir into the bread-milk mixture. Pour into a buttered 2-quart baking dish. Bake about 50 minutes, or until the top is set and springs back from gentle pressure. Remove and set aside.

To make the berry sauce, melt 1 tablespoon butter in a large skillet over medium-high heat. Add the strawberries and cook about 5 minutes, or until they give up their liquid. Add the sugar and lemon juice and cook about 2 minutes, or until the strawberries soften. Add the raspberries and remaining butter. Cook just until the raspberries are soft and warm. Serve bowls of the bread pudding with the hot berry sauce.

Yield: 8 servings

Note: *Unsweetened frozen berries may be substituted for fresh.*

POACHED PEARS WITH SAGE AND CINNAMON CRÈME FRAÎCHE

.... ❖ ....

This pear dessert is great-tasting hot or cold, and it keeps well for a week in the refrigerator. It is simmered in wine, spices, and sage, which has a musky-mint flavor. Because sage is fairly cold-hardy, you can harvest fresh sage almost year-round if protected with a cold frame. Use pears that are ripe but still slightly firm so they keep their shape. A zinfandel or Rhone wine is especially good to use.

I n a large saucepan, combine the wine, ½ cup sugar, sage, allspice, cloves, cinnamon stick, star anise, and cardamom pods. Bring to a boil over medium-high heat, then reduce heat to low and simmer for 5 minutes. Set aside to cool.

When the liquid has cooled, core the pears with an apple corer or thin knife, peel, and drop each one immediately into the spiced wine. Make sure they can all stand without touching and that the wine covers them. Bring to a simmer over medium heat, then cover and reduce heat to low. Cook for about 30 minutes, or until the pears are tender. Remove the pan from the heat and let the pears cool in the wine for at least 6 hours.

When ready to serve, mix the crème fraîche, cinnamon, and the remaining 3 tablespoons sugar in a small bowl. Alternately, combine yogurt and cinnamon. Divide the crème fraîche or yogurt among six small plates or bowls. Put a pear in the center, and garnish each with a fresh sage leaf in the top. The leftover wine may be heated and served as mulled wine.

Yield: 6 servings

4 cups dry red wine
½ cup plus 3 tablespoons sugar
   Four 4-inch sprigs fresh sage
8 allspice berries
10 whole cloves
   One 3-inch cinnamon stick
1 whole star anise
8 cardamom pods
6 cooking pears, such as Anjou, Bartlett, or Bosc
1 cup crème fraîche (see box on page 122), or 1 cup vanilla nonfat yogurt
1 teaspoon ground cinnamon

He who plant pears
Plants food for his heirs.

— Anonymous

SWEET HERB BOUQUET GARNI

To make a sweet herb bouquet garni, for cooking desserts, tie together a sprig each of sweet cicely, angelica, lemon verbena, and lemon thyme with a piece of kitchen twine. Add to the saucepan when cooking sugar syrup or fruit or when scalding milk for pudding or dessert sauces. Remove after cooking. Other herbs may be used; bay leaf is especially noted for flavoring custard sauce.

MANGO-PAPAYA-MINT MOUSSE

❖

1 cup ½-inch mango cubes
1 cup ½-inch papaya cubes
2 tablespoons sugar
½ cup fresh mint leaves
1 tablespoon lemon juice
¼ cup orange juice
1 tablespoon unflavored gelatin
½ cup vanilla nonfat yogurt

Transport yourself to a tropical spa with this exotic, yet low-calorie, flummery. If you cannot find fully ripe fruit, buy them unripe and keep in a closed paper bag at room temperature for several days.

In a large bowl, combine the mango, papaya, sugar, mint, and 1 tablespoon lemon juice. Let sit for 1 hour.

In a small saucepan, combine the orange juice and gelatin. Cook over low heat, stirring constantly, until gelatin is dissolved.

Put the fruit in a blender and purée on low speed. With the blender running, gradually pour in the gelatin mixture. Pour into a bowl and cool.

In a small bowl, whip the yogurt with a whisk or mixer for about 3 minutes, until light and fluffy. Fold the yogurt into the fruit purée. Serve immediately or chilled.

Yield: 4 to 6 servings

*Down by a little path I fonde
Of mintes full and fennel green.*

— Geoffrey Chaucer

LEMON BASIL SNAPS WITH PISTACHIOS

Reading the Shepherd's garden seeds catalog is a pleasure in itself, but it also offers tempting recipes that focus on vegetables and herbs. These and other recipes have been collected in several cookbooks, including More Recipes from a Kitchen Garden. *Among the delectable ideas from authors Renee Shepherd and Fran Raboff is this buttery cookie, tart with lemon and spicy with basil. If lemon basil is unavailable, use plain basil instead.*

  2 **cups unbleached or all-purpose flour**
½ **teaspoon baking soda**
¼ **teaspoon salt**
¾ **cup (1½ sticks) butter, at room temperature**
¾ **cup plus 3 tablespoons sugar**
  1 **large egg, or ¼ cup egg substitute**
  1 **tablespoon minced zest of lemon**
  1 **tablespoon lemon juice**
⅓ **cup minced fresh lemon basil leaves**
⅓ **cup finely chopped, shelled pistachio nuts**

Sift flour, baking soda, and salt into a large bowl. In another bowl, cream the butter and ¾ cup sugar until light and fluffy. Beat in the egg or egg substitute. Add the lemon zest, lemon juice, and lemon basil. Gradually add flour mixture to creamed mixture, mixing well after each addition. Cover and refrigerate for 1 hour, or until mixture is firm.

Heat oven to 350°F. In a small dish, combine pistachios with 3 tablespoons sugar. Shape the chilled dough into 1-inch balls. Roll the balls in sugar-nut mixture until coated. Place 2 inches apart on ungreased baking sheets. Flatten cookies slightly with the palm of your hand. Bake for 10 to 12 minutes, or until golden. Transfer to racks to cool.

Yield: 4 dozen cookies

STRAWBERRY-RHUBARB CRUNCH
WITH ROSE GERANIUM

························ ❖ ························

¼ cup orange juice

3 tablespoons minced fresh rose geranium leaves

2 pounds fresh rhubarb, cut into 1-inch pieces

1½ cups fresh strawberries

2 teaspoons minced zest of orange

1 teaspoon rose water (optional)

½ cup rose geranium sugar (see Herb Sugar recipe)

3 tablespoons cornstarch

¾ cup old-fashioned rolled oats

½ cup unbleached or all-purpose flour

½ cup firmly packed brown sugar

¼ cup (½ stick) butter, at room temperature

½ cup chopped, toasted walnuts

Bursting with the flavors of the spring fruit garden, this velvety dessert with an exotic hint of roses is tantalizing.

In a small saucepan, heat orange juice with 2 tablespoons rose geranium leaves just until warm. Cover and steep for 15 minutes. Heat oven to 350°F. Coat a 9-inch square baking pan or 1½- or 2-quart baking dish with nonstick cooking spray.

In a large bowl, combine rhubarb and strawberries. Stir in orange juice–rose geranium mixture, orange zest, and rose water, if using. Add rose geranium sugar and cornstarch, combining well. Pour into baking pan or dish.

In a bowl, combine rolled oats, flour, brown sugar, and remaining 1 tablespoon rose geranium leaves. With your fingers, work the butter into the oat mixture until it resembles coarse meal. Stir in the walnuts.

Spread topping over fruit, lightly patting down, and bake for 50 to 60 minutes, or until golden and bubbly. Serve warm with vanilla ice cream.

Yield: 8 servings

HERB SUGAR

Add a subtle yet distinct essence to desserts or tea by using sugar flavored with herbs or edible flowers.

Rose geranium leaves, lavender flowers, and rose petals are the old-fashioned favorites for flavoring sugar, but consider other herbs and flowers, such as clove pinks, mints, lemon verbena, bee balm, anise hyssop, sweet cicely, or angelica.

Dry the leaves or petals for one day, then layer them with either granulated or confectioners sugar in an airtight jar. Remove the herbs or flowers before using, or create an herb-sugar mixture by whirling in a food processor until the herbs are finely ground.

Dianthus, *signifying the Flower of God, or divine flower; so named on account of its preeminent beauty. . . . The fragrance of some of the species is peculiarly grateful, and no plant in this respect surpasses the Clove Pink.*

— Joseph Breck, *Breck's Book of Flowers*

BABA CAKES WITH CLOVE PINKS

Little sponge cakes leavened with yeast and soaked in sugar syrup spiced with clove pinks harken to Elizabethan times. A forerunner of the florist carnation, clove pinks were Chaucer's "sops in wine." Crystallize the petals for garnishes or use them in fruit dishes, sandwiches, soups, sauces, vinegar, liqueur, or wine. Be sure to remove the bitter white "heel" on the bottom of each petal.

1 package active dry yeast
½ cup very warm (105°–110°F) water
1¾ cups unbleached or all-purpose flour
4 large eggs, or 1 cup egg substitute, at room temperature
¼ cup sugar, preferably flavored with clove pinks
2 tablespoons minced fresh clove pink flowers
½ teaspoon ground cloves
¼ teaspoon salt
½ cup (1 stick) butter, at room temperature
2 cups Herb Syrup flavored with clove pinks (see recipe)

In a large bowl, combine yeast and water. Let sit for 5 minutes. Add ½ cup flour and mix well with an electric mixer. Beat in the eggs, one at a time, or the egg substitute, ¼ cup at a time. Add the sugar, clove pinks, cloves, salt, and remaining flour, beating until smooth. Cover loosely with wax paper or plastic wrap and let rise in a warm place until doubled in bulk. Adding 1 tablespoon at a time, beat butter into the risen batter.

Butter standard-sized muffin pans. Put 3 tablespoons of batter into each cup, cover loosely, and let sit for 45 minutes.

While the batter is rising, heat oven to 400°F. Bake the cakes for about 20 minutes, or until golden. Let cool in the pan for a few minutes, then remove the cakes and set in a single layer in a pan. Pour the syrup over the top and let sit for 1 hour.

Set on wax paper, bottom side up. Serve with sweetened whipped cream and fresh or crystallized clove pink petals.

Yield: Twelve 2½-inch cakes

HERB SYRUP

Apricots poached in fennel syrup, lemon sorbet with lavender syrup, blueberry pancakes with lemon thyme syrup, or baba cakes with clove pink syrup are just a few ways that herb syrups can highlight foods.

1 cup herb leaves or edible flowers
2 cups sugar

First, make an infusion by bringing 3 cups of water to a boil. Remove from heat and stir in 1 cup herb leaves or edible flowers. Cover and steep for 30 minutes. Strain out the herbs or flowers. Return liquid to the pan and stir in 2 cups sugar. Bring to a boil and cook for 10 minutes. Cool and bottle. Stored in the refrigerator, this will keep for several months.

For a variation, substitute a fruit juice for some or all of the water, reducing the sugar if desired.

ALMOND AND LAVENDER CONFECTIONS

❖

Since antiquity, sugared almonds and sweetmeats, or comfits, of flowers and seeds have been part of the most sumptuous of feasts. These confections of almond paste and lavender flowers carry on that tradition.

One 7-ounce package almond paste
¼ **cup lavender flowers**
¼ **cup ground almonds**
½ **teaspoon minced zest of orange**

In a small bowl, combine almond paste and lavender flowers using your fingers. Form into ¾-inch balls. In a flat dish, combine ground almonds and orange zest. Roll each ball in the almond mixture. Place in small candy cups.
Yield: 25 candies

CRYSTALLIZED FLOWERS AND LEAVES

A favorite Victorian conceit was to decorate cakes, puddings, and other desserts with crystallized violets, rose petals, and mint leaves. A supply of these kept on hand turns even the plainest sweet into a whimsical delight.

Besides violets, consider using other members of the viola family such as Johnny-jump-ups. Whole miniature rose blossoms as well as rose petals can also be cystallized. Or, use the leaves of various mints, especially chocolate mint. Consider clove pinks and other edible flowers, too.

To crystallize 1 cup of flowers and leaves, beat 1 large egg white, at room temperature, until frothy. With a small clean artist's brush, completely coat all sides of each flower or leaf, one at a time. Immediately sprinkle each side with superfine sugar. Place on a cake rack or screen placed over a baking sheet. Let dry thoroughly in a cool, dry place. Store in an airtight container.

Lavender

It is golden maxim to cultivate the garden for the nose, and the eyes will take care of themselves.

— Robert Louis Stevenson

Tropical Cooler with Pineapple Sage and Mint (page 132) ▶

Drinks

TROPICAL COOLER WITH PINEAPPLE SAGE AND MINT

.... ❖ ....

1½ cups water
¼ cup fresh pineapple sage leaves
¼ cup fresh mint leaves
1 tablespoon minced fresh ginger
2 cups pineapple juice, chilled
1½ cups papaya nectar, chilled
1 cup orange juice, chilled
¼ cup lime juice
1 quart sparkling mineral water

The bright red flowers of pineapple sage are beloved by hummingbirds and herb gardeners alike. The leaves have a wonderful aroma of pineapple that — when combined with mint, ginger, and tropical juices — makes a lovely summer drink. If pineapple sage flowers are available, freeze some in ice cubes made from distilled water or serve glasses of the cooler with sprigs of the flowers.

Bring water to a boil and pour over the pineapple sage and mint leaves and fresh ginger in a heat-proof bowl. Steep for 15 minutes. Strain and discard the herbs. In a pitcher, combine herb liquid with the pineapple, papaya, orange, and lime juices. Just before serving, add sparkling water. Serve immediately, garnished with fresh pineapple sage or mint sprigs.
Yield: 2½ quarts

USING PINEAPPLE SAGE

Pineapple sage is rapidly becoming a favorite among herb lovers. Adored for its strongly pineapple-scented-and-flavored leaves, this herb can only be used fresh. Add it to green and fruit salads, butters, and drinks. Be sure to make plenty of pineapple sage sorbets, vinegars, and sugars to buoy you through the winter months.

FLOWER ICE CUBES

Edible flowers imbedded in ice cubes or an ice ring are a charming conceit for chilled drinks or punches. Use any edible flower such as borage, clove pinks, lavender, nasturtium, mint, pineapple sage, rose geranium, rose petals, thyme, or violets. Distilled water yields clear ice, but tap water can also be used.

To make, put an individual flower or cluster in each section of an ice cube tray. Fill halfway with water. Freeze solid; then fill completely with water and freeze.

LAVENDER-BASIL PUNCH

❖

For those averse to sickeningly sweet party drinks, this unusually flavored punch lends a sophisticated touch to any gathering. If your lavender is abundant, decorate the bowl, pitcher handle, or punch ladle with little bouquets.

Combine water, cinnamon, cloves, and allspice in a saucepan and bring to a boil over high heat. Reduce heat to low and simmer for 5 minutes. Remove from heat, stir in cinnamon basil and lavender flowers, cover, and steep for 15 mintues. Strain into a pitcher, removing spices and lavender. Stir in grape juice, lemon juice, and sugar. Cover and refrigerate. Just before serving, pour into a punch bowl or large pitcher; add lemon slices, ice, and sparkling water. Serve immediately.
Yield: 2 quarts

2 cups water
One 3-inch cinnamon stick
½ teaspoon whole cloves
½ teaspoon whole allspice
½ cup fresh cinnamon basil leaves
¼ cup lavender flowers
2 cups purple grape juice
½ cup lemon juice
¾ cup sugar
1 lemon, thinly sliced
1 quart sparkling mineral water

CRANBERRY PUNCH WITH LAVENDER AND ROSEMARY

❖

Use this recipe as a basis for experimenting with other fruit juices and herbs. Health-food stores abound with juices not often seen in groceries, but don't overlook basics such as pineapple juice or the different cranberry mixtures. Other herbs that work well in drinks include the various mints, lemon balm, lemongrass, lemon verbena, angelica, sweet cicely, various thymes, cinnamon and lemon basils, borage, parsley, and fennel.

Combine the rosemary, lavender, cinnamon, and cloves in a small saucepan with 2½ cups water. Bring to a boil over high heat, then reduce heat to low and simmer for 5 minutes. Remove from the heat and let steep for 5 minutes. Strain and combine with the juice in a pitcher. Refrigerate and serve cold, or heat and serve warm.
Yield: 1½ quarts

¼ cup fresh rosemary leaves
1 tablespoon dried lavender flowers
2 cinnamon sticks
6 whole cloves
1 quart cranberry juice

As Rosemary is to the Spirit, so Lavender is to the Soul.

— Anonymous

TROPICAL SMOOTHIE WITH MINT AND LEMON BALM

Mint and lemon balm embroider the splendor of this healthful refreshment, be it for breakfast or a snack.

  1 medium banana, peeled and sliced
  1 medium mango, peeled, seeded, and chopped
  1 medium papaya, peeled, seeded, and chopped
  3 cups skim milk
  ¼ cup fresh mint leaves
  ¼ cup fresh lemon balm leaves
  2 tablespoons honey

Combine all ingredients in a blender, purée, and serve immediately. Garnish with sprigs of fresh mint or lemon balm, if desired.

Yield: 1 quart

ORANGE, MELON, AND BORAGE COOLER

Not the most graceful of plants in the garden, borage has leaves with a flavor reminiscent of cucumber and star-shaped blue flowers that more than transcend any other imperfections. This drink is so delicious it hardly seems fair that it should also be low in fat and high in vitamins. Canteloupe, crenshaw, and honeydew melons may all be used, alone or in combination. If using all watermelon, reduce the ice cubes to four.

  3 cups melon chunks, seeds removed
  1 cup orange juice
  2 tablespoons sugar
  8 ice cubes
  ½ cup plain nonfat yogurt
  2 cups small, tender fresh borage leaves

Combine all ingredients in a blender, purée, and serve immediately. Garnish with fresh borage flowers, if desired.

Yield: 1 quart

Lemon balm

The charm of balm as a garden plant, aside from its interesting history, is the delicious lemony, minty scent from its leaves. If grown on a bank where one can stroke it in passing, it is always a delight to sniff its fragrance on one's fingers.

— Helen Morgenthau Fox, *Gardening with Herbs*

LEMON VERBENA ICED TEA

❖

Favored by the French, lemon verbena tea is used for everything from entertaining to curing the common cold. Refreshing yet caffeine-free, this version may also be made with dried leaves, reducing the amount by one-half.

2 quarts boiling water
1 cup fresh lemon verbena leaves
1 cup orange juice

Put the leaves in a heatproof container and pour the water over them. Let steep for 45 minutes. Strain and cool. Add the orange juice just before serving over ice.

Yield: 2 quarts

RED WINE COOLER WITH LEMON BALM AND LEMON THYME

❖

Lemony, with just a touch of mint, lemon balm shines in drinks, salads, and any uncooked foods. The genus name Melissa *is from the Greek for "honeybee," and this refreshing punch is certainly touched by the balmy sweetness.*

1 bottle dry or medium-dry white wine
1 cup orange juice
¼ cup lemon or lime juice
1 cup chopped fresh lemon balm leaves
3 tablespoons fresh lemon thyme leaves
½ cup brandy
¼ cup honey
1 quart sparkling mineral water

Combine wine, orange and lemon or lime juices, lemon balm, lemon thyme, brandy, and honey in a large glass pitcher or jug. Stir to mix, cover, and refrigerate for at least 4 hours. Strain and add mineral water. Serve over ice, garnished with sprigs of lemon balm.

HERBAL WINE

Wine flavored with herbs or edible flowers makes a delightful change of pace for an aperitif or for a chilled drink on a summer afternoon. Herbs will not improve a poor-quality wine, so choose a good white, rosé, or light red. Add three or four sprigs of fresh herbs or a handful of flowers to the bottle, recork, and let steep for at least 8 hours in a cool, dark place. Filter before serving.

Some of the herbs and edible flowers suitable for flavoring wine are borage, lemon balm, lemon verbena, marjoram, rosemary, angelica, certain mints, tarragon, any of the basils, lemon thyme, lavender, rose petals, rose geranium, and clove pinks. A strip of orange or lemon zest is sometimes a good addition.

Lovage

❖

THE LEAVES AND STEMS of lovage enhance salads, soups, stews, and sauces. The fresh stems and roots can also be cooked as a vegetable or candied. Use the seeds, crushed or ground, in pickles, cheese dips and spreads, breads, salad dressings, and sauces. Consider using lovage with carrots, cabbage, potatoes, tomatoes, beans, poultry, grains, and salt-free herb seasoning.

Harvest the young leaves or side shoots of lovage all summer long; the best flavor occurs before flowering. For winter use, dry or freeze the leaves. Collect seed heads when they start to turn brown. Harvest the roots in the fall when the plants are at least 3 years old.

Native to southern Europe, lovage has been grown in gardens since antiquity. Its popularity reached a height during the Middle Ages, when it was favored for both culinary and medicinal purposes ranging from lightening freckles to relieving indigestion and sore throats. The ancient Greeks and Romans as well as the Tudors and Stuarts used it as a bath herb. Lovage was also recommended for love potions, hence its name.

LOVAGE BLOODY MARY

❖

Lovage provides a celery "taste-alike" from your garden, giving Bloody Marys an extra depth of flavor and pizzazz.

1½ **cups vodka**
  6 **cups tomato juice**
½ **cup lemon or lime juice**
  4 **teaspoons grated horseradish, fresh or preserved in vinegar**
  2 **tablespoons Worcestershire sauce**
  1 **teaspoon hot red pepper sauce**
  1 **teaspoon sugar**
  3 **large fresh lovage stalks with leaves**

Combine all ingredients in a large pitcher, bruising the lovage by hand as you put it in. Let steep for 20 minutes, then remove the lovage. Serve over ice, with a small lovage stalk in each glass if desired.
Yield: 2 quarts

AQUAVIT

❖

Literally translated as "water of life," Scandinavian aquavit is best known as commercially available neutral grain spirits flavored with caraway. But, since time immemorial people of all countries and persuasions have flavored spirits at home with herbs and spices. This recipe exemplifies one of the many possibilities of such personal creations.

1 whole star anise
8 allspice berries
2 whole cloves
4 stalks fresh caraway
4 stalks fresh fennel
One 750-ml bottle less ¼ cup high-quality vodka

Preheat oven to 375°F. Toast the star anise, allspice, and cloves in a small baking pan for 8 minutes, stirring occasionally, until fragrant. Put the toasted spices, caraway, and fennel in the vodka bottle. Cap the bottle and let stand in a warm place for two days. Make sure that the herbs stay submerged in the vodka.

After two days, pour off a tiny bit and taste — it should be light green and richly herbal. If not, recap and let stand for several more days. When the taste is to your liking, decant through a strainer or coffee filter into another bottle. Store in the freezer and serve ice cold in small glasses, perhaps as an accompaniment to gravlax.
Yield: One 690-ml bottle

HERBAL LIQUEUR

The distilling and flavoring of strong spirits with herbs dates to the 1500s when monks began making them for sale. Two of the best known commercial herbal liqueurs, Benedictine and Chartreuse, carry on the monastic tradition. They are blends of more than 50 and 230 herbs, respectively.

To make an herbal liqueur, coarsely chop ½ to ⅔ cup fresh leaves or flowers. Place in a sterilized glass jar and add 2 cups alcohol such as vodka or brandy. Attach the lid and steep for at least a day, or longer if the flavor is not strong enough.

Strain the mixture through a coffee filter or several layers of cheesecloth. Make a sugar syrup by mixing 2 parts sugar with 1 part water, then boiling until the sugar is dissolved. Cool before using. Add ⅔ cup sugar syrup, or to taste. Add 1 tablespoon glycerine, if desired, to thicken. (Glycerine may be purchased at drug stores or wine-making supply shops.) Pour into a sterilized bottle and cork. Let mature in a cool, dark place for at least a month.

Herb leaves and seeds and edible flowers used to flavor liqueurs include angelica, anise, bay, burnet, caraway, clove pinks, coriander, cumin, fennel, hyssop, lavender, lemon balm, lemon verbena, marjoram, mints, rose petals, rose geranium, rosemary, saffron, sage, savory, sweet cicely, sweet woodruff, tarragon, thyme, and violets. Spices and citrus zest may also be added.

MULLED HERBAL CIDER

*The thyme strong scented
    'neath our feet,
The Marjoram beds so
    doubly sweet,
And pennyroyal's creeping
    twine
These, each succeeding each
    one thine.*

— from Mrs. C. F. Leyel's *Herbal Delights*

For autumn gatherings, flavor fresh apple cider with herbs instead of spices. Serve with fresh apple cake or pumpkin pie.

Four 4-inch sprigs fresh rosemary
Four 4-inch sprigs fresh thyme
Four 4-inch sprigs fresh sage
2 quarts fresh apple cider

Combine rosemary, thyme, sage, and cider in a nonreactive saucepan and bring to a boil over high heat. Reduce heat to low and simmer for 10 minutes. Serve immediately.
Yield: 2 quarts

FRUIT OR VEGETABLE JUICES WITH HERBS

JUICE-HERB COMBINATIONS

**Apple juice with sage
    or thyme**
Berry juice with mint
**Carrot juice with marjoram
    or burnet**
**Celery juice with lovage, parsley,
    or chives**
Cherry juice with lavender
**Cranberry juice with ginger
    or rosemary**
Grape juice with thyme
**Grapefruit juice with angelica
    or sweet cicely**
Papaya juice with marjoram
**Peach or nectarine juice with
    coriander**
Raspberry juice with rose geranium
Tomato juice with basil

Appetizing and healthful, fruit and vegetable juices are refreshing on their own, but with the addition of herbs, they provide even more pleasure and health-giving properties.

With an electric juice extractor, add herbs as the juice is being made or afterward. For store-bought juices, add fresh herbs 30 minutes before serving.
Use 1 teaspoon of fresh herbs for 1 cup of juice.

FRUIT PROTEIN SHAKE WITH LEMON BALM

❖

½ cup fresh soft fruit, such as peaches, blueberries, strawberries,
   raspberries, papaya, or pineapple
¼ cup low-fat soft tofu
½ ripe medium banana
½ cup skim milk
2 tablespoons lemon balm leaves
1 tablespoon honey
2 ice cubes

In a blender, combine all ingredients until smooth.
Serve immediately.

Yield: 1 serving

MOCHA-MINT CAPPUCCINO SHAKE

❖

*Think of this as a low-calorie candy bar with the wonderful flavors of coffee,
chocolate, and mint.*

½ cup nonfat coffee yogurt
½ ripe medium banana
¼ cup skim milk
2 tablespoons fresh mint leaves
1 teaspoon cocoa powder
2 ice cubes
   Dash of cinnamon

In a blender, combine all ingredients until smooth.
Serve immediately.

Yield: 1 serving

Lemon Balm

NATIVE TO CENTRAL and southern Europe, northern Africa, and western Asia, lemon balm is surrounded with much lore and legend. It has been associated with strengthening the mind, calming nerves, promoting longevity, and healing wounds.

The Latin name for lemon balm, *Melissa*, derives from the Greek word for "honeybee," referring to the love that bees have for the flower's nectar. It is said that lemon balm will attract new bees and calm restive ones if a beehive is rubbed with the herb or if it grows nearby.

Lemon balm has a strong flavor of lemon intermingled with a bit of mint. Producing an abundance of foliage, lemon balm is used in hot or iced teas, summer drinks, fruit punches, green or fruit salads, herb cheeses, and with fish and vegetables. The delicate flavor dissipates quickly with cooking, so it's best to add it at the last minute or not cook it at all.

Besides adding a lemony zest to food, lemon balm is excellent in potpourris, herbal sleep pillows, and herbal baths.

Herb Tea Punch

1 cup fresh mint leaves
1 cup fresh borage leaves
¼ cup fresh gingerroot, peeled
    and minced
4 cups boiling water
1 cup lemon juice
1 cup orange juice
1 cup pineapple juice
4 cups Earl Grey tea
1 cup corn syrup
3 quarts sparkling mineral water
    Borage blossoms and calendula
    petals

For a special party or summer afternoon tea, this punch flavored with tingly mint, cucumber-like borage, and spicy ginger is sure to slake parched throats.

Combine mint, borage, and ginger in a nonreactive, heatproof bowl or saucepan. Pour boiling water over the top and let steep for 20 minutes. Strain and pour into a large bowl, pitcher, or saucepan. Add lemon, orange, and pineapple juices, tea, and corn syrup. Chill for at least 4 hours. When ready to serve, combine the mixture with mineral water and serve immediately. Garnish with fresh borage blossoms and calendula petals.

Yield: 32 servings

HERBAL TEA

No doubt herbal teas have been around since Homo sapiens first boiled water. Throughout the ages we have benefited not only from their natural therapeutic effects but also from the soothing ritual of preparing and drinking them. Calorie- and caffeine-free, herbal teas offer us subtle, delicate flavors and aromas.

Every part of thousands of plants has been used in herbal teas, but with home-grown herbs, the leaves, flowers, and seeds are most often used. To properly make herbal tea, use a china pot warmed first with hot water. Use 1 teaspoon dried herbs or 1 tablespoon fresh herbs for each cup of boiling water. Iced herbal teas are usually made stronger. Also, herbs such as lemon balm and lemon verbena may be added to black or green tea. Steep the tea for 5 to 10 minutes, using a tea cosy to maintain the tea's warmth. For a stronger tea, use more herbs — not a longer steeping time, which may make the tea bitter. Herbal teas are usually drunk without milk but may be sweetened with honey.

The following herbs and edible flowers may be used separately or in various combinations: anise, basil, bee balm, borage, caraway, catnip, chamomile, coriander, dill, fennel, ginger, hyssop, lavender, lemon balm, lemongrass, lemon verbena, lovage, marjoram, mints, parsley, pineapple sage, rose geranium, rosemary, sage, and thyme.

Borage

Terracotta pots offer several advantages for herb growing: ▶
They are porous, making for good drainage, and come in
a wide variety of shapes and sizes.

Herb Gardening
in Containers,
Outdoors and In

There's very little new under the sun. Early records show that the ancient Greeks, Romans, and Egyptians grew bay, myrtle, and other herbs in clay pots. The Moors of southern Spain were known for their lavish use of containers in courtyard gardens. Illustrated manuscripts from Britain as early as the twelfth century show potted plants in monastery and palace gardens. The classicism of fifteenth- and sixteenth-century Italian gardens greatly relied on ornate stone and lead planters. With industrialization, Victorian and Edwardian gardeners had a plethora of elaborate containers from which to choose, ranging from cast-iron urns to those made of stone, lead, and terracotta. Planted with an ever-expanding array of tender plants, the conservatories and pristine lawns of these eras were brightened with exuberant pots of colorful flowers.

Today, container gardening is once more in the throes of a renaissance. For some this is due to the limitations of space in high-rises and condominiums; for others it may be due to the ease and accessibility of gardening in containers. Ultimately, people simply appreciate what has been known since antiquity: pots overflowing with plants add beauty and dimension to the landscape. Best of all, container gardening is an ideal way to easily grow all the herbs you might want for cooking.

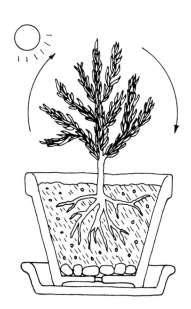

Every herb needs sunlight, air circulation, and well-drained soil to grow in a container.

WHAT HERBS NEED

In terms of growing herbs, container gardening is a method that truly goes hand-in-trowel. All of the many pages written on the growing of herbs can be reduced to three major factors that most herbs need to grow well: lots of sunlight, plenty of air circulation, and well-drained soil that is kept a little on the dry side. Growing herbs in containers and small raised beds readily meets these criteria. As a result, herbs grown in containers often do much better than those grown in the garden.

Standard Soil Mix

After sun, air, and soil moisture, the most important single element necessary for the success of container gardening is the soil mix. Plants grow best when their root systems are able to easily spread through the soil, getting the right balance of water, air, and nutrients. Too much or too little of any one will result in unhealthy or dead plants. Sal's many years of growing millions of herb plants at his nursery have yielded a recommended soil mix based on equal parts of four ingredients: topsoil, coarse perlite, peat moss, and coarse sand. Each of these items can be purchased at most garden supply stores.

The topsoil should be of good quality — either from your own garden or, preferably, sterilized topsoil available in bags at garden centers. Perlite is volcanic pumice. It loosens the soil and keeps it from becoming compacted. Be sure to buy coarse perlite. Do not substitute vermiculite for the perlite, as herbs do not grow well in it. Peat moss adds humus to the soil. One of the best kinds is the very fibrous New Brunswick blonde peat. Alternatives to peat moss include expandable blocks of coconut fiber, and homemade or purchased compost. The final ingredient is coarse sand or fine gravel, which ensures good drainage and soil aeration. Chicken or turkey grit can be substituted.

Fertilizers and pH

You may have read that herbs grow in poor soil, but the reality is that they respond well to some fertilization. A simple organic method of feeding is to use dehydrated cow manure and bonemeal. Both are widely available at garden centers. To one bushel of standard potting soil, add a generous cupful each of manure and bone meal; mix it in thoroughly. Worth seeking out is either worm or cricket "compost" instead of the cow manure.

Alternatively, consider using one of the various complete organic or natural fertilizers that are commercially available. Use at the manufacturer's recommended rate.

Because container plantings are watered frequently, the nutrients get washed away from the roots more quickly than in the garden. It is advisable to feed at least once a week when plants are actively growing. Either scratch granular organic fertilizer into the soil surface, or water with a soluble organic fertilizer, if desired. With either method, follow the manufacturer's recommendations. The easiest method is to choose what is called a "complete fertilizer" — one that contains nitrogen, phosphorus, and potassium, as indicated by the three numbers on the bag. You can also mix your own from individual components.

Fertilizers containing kelp or other seaweed and fish emulsion seem to particularly benefit plants; an excellent brand available by mail-order includes enzymes, vitamins and minerals, liquid humus, marine algae, and chelating agents.

The pH of a soil reflects the hydrogen ion concentration and affects nutrient uptake. The pH is based on a scale of 1 to 14, with 7 being neutral; numbers below 7 indicate an increasingly acidic soil and numbers above 7 indicate an increasingly alkaline soil. Most herbs grow in a pH range of 6 to 7, which is provided with Sal's recommended soil mixture described on page 142. If you want to be

WORM COMPOST

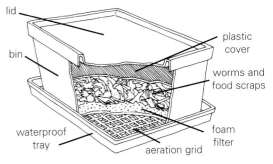

lid
plastic cover
bin
worms and food scraps
waterproof tray
foam filter
aeration grid

You can recycle plant-matter kitchen scraps and feed your plants as well with worm compost. Mail-order sources carry special bins, starter worms, and a how-to book for producing this nutritious soil amendment and fertilizer in your basement or garage.

BAG-A-POT

While the soil is not as good as Sal's mixture (described on page 142), an inexpensive and easy way to "container" garden is by purchasing a bag of potting soil, laying it flat on the ground, and cutting several small holes in the bottom and 3-inch holes at 8- to 12-inch intervals in the top. Plant in these larger holes. Feed and water regularly.

Plain terracotta pots can be decorated with acrylic craft paints to accent both the landscape and the plants. The pots should be clean and dry. The paint may be diluted with a little water and sponged on, perhaps with several layers of colors, allowing each layer to dry first. Or, paint with the name of an herb on the rim and decorate the body of the pot with a likeness of the herb.

Wooden containers do not break when they freeze. Before planting, drill ½-inch holes in the bottom of the wooden containers every eight to ten inches.

sure, you can check the soil pH before planting and then occasionally throughout the growing season. Inexpensive test kits or pH meters are available at garden centers. To make a soil more alkaline, thoroughly mix in some dolomitic lime; to make a soil more acidic, mix in some elemental sulfur powder.

CONTAINERS AND SMALL RAISED BEDS

The range of containers available, either commercially or from found objects, is staggering. Of these, the two best materials for growing herbs are those that are porous. This narrows the range to containers made of terracotta and wood. Although plastic and fiberglass pots are lightweight, their non-porous nature causes them to dry out more slowly than porous containers. If you want to experiment with non-porous containers, go ahead, but put most of your money and effort into wood and terracotta.

Terracotta

Although terracotta pots are generally preferred for herbs, they have several disadvantages. Besides their cost and weight, clay pots are likely to crack and break in freezing weather. To circumvent this, they must either be emptied and turned upside down or the planted container stored in a garage or basement over the winter.

Another problem with clay is that in the heat of summer a terracotta pot can get very hot and dry out very quickly, especially if it is set on brick, stone, concrete, or asphalt. Because plant roots grow to the outside of the root ball, the heat and dry conditions can damage them. To alleviate this problem, raise the pot several inches above the surface or double-pot by inserting one container inside another and filling in between with long-fibered sphagnum moss.

Containers of herbs can easily be moved around to provide accents on a patio where desired.

HERB BOX DESIGNS

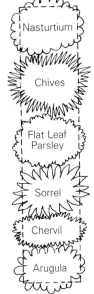

Nasturtium

Chives

Flat Leaf Parsley

Sorrel

Chervil

Arugula

Suggested planting plan for a salad herb box. You could also fill a box with varieties of just one herb, such as basil.

Below: Suggested planting plan for a box of kitchen herbs. Santolina is added as an insect repellent to protect the other herbs.

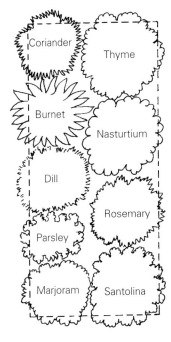

Coriander

Thyme

Burnet

Nasturtium

Dill

Parsley

Rosemary

Marjoram

Santolina

Wood

Wooden containers offer certain advantages. They do not heat up as much as clay, and they do not freeze and break. Containers made of redwood or cedar are very long-lasting. Those made of spruce or pine will deteriorate after two to five years, depending on the conditions. Treated wood should not be used for growing edibles, as there is potential harm from the chemicals used. If you want to treat the wood yourself, use a preservative called Woodlife.

In general, choose larger pots over smaller ones. Most individual herbs should be planted in pots 12 to 14 inches in diameter and about 12 inches deep. Larger containers require less water and, consequently, less fertilizing. Containers for mixed plantings are best at 24 to 36 inches in diameter.

Small Raised Beds

Small raised beds lack the mobility of containers but otherwise are able to meet the basic growing criteria. An area only 4 or 6 feet square readily accommodates 8 to 10 herbs. Mail-order garden supply companies and local garden centers offer a variety of units that can be set up quickly with little or no do-it-yourself skills.

Planting a Window Box

MATERIALS

- Wire hayrack planter
- Sphagnum moss (enough to line inside of planter)
- Large black plastic bag or coir fiber
- Multipurpose potting soil
- Plants of your choice

The concept of growing herbs in window boxes is an idyllic one, complete with scents wafting through the screen. The reality is that most commercially available windowboxes are too small for productive growth. It is better to have them specially made, with a depth of at least 10 inches. Such a size will make the box very heavy, so be sure to attach it securely to the house. An alternative is to use a wire "hayrack" planter lined with coir fiber or plastic, planted as follows.

1. Push the sphagnum moss down over the bottom and sides of the wire planter, covering the whole frame. If using a coir liner, insert it into frame.

2. If you're using a plastic liner, pierce the bottom of it with scissors to make drainage holes. Cut several holes in the front and each side of the plastic bag.

3. Select flowers to hang along the front and sides of window; insert them from outside through the layer of moss and into the holes in the plastic bag or between pieces of coir fiber.

4. Fill the interior of the planter with a layer of potting soil and add plants to the middle and upper sides, covering roots with the soil. Build the inner plantings, adding more potting soil as needed. Make sure the planting is well balanced and proportioned.

Combining herbs and flowers in a window box delights the senses.

An abandoned boat makes an appropriate container for a seaside deck garden.

HERB BARREL DESIGNS

Suggested planting plan for kitchen herbs in a round wooden barrel. You can tailor barrels to fit your tastes and needs. A "tea tub" could include anise hyssop, spearmint, lemon balm, and lemon verbena.

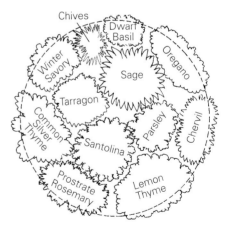

Suggested planting plan for a larger barrel. Once again, santolina is added as a natural insect repellent.

ACQUIRING PLANTS

Many herbs are readily started from seed, but because you'll probably want no more than several plants of each herb for container growing, it's much easier to purchase small herb plants. A wide range of herbs are offered at many garden centers. Local herb societies and groups often have special herb sales in the spring, offering unusual varieties. There is also a wealth of excellent and reliable mail-order sources for herbs.

If you must start your herbs from seed, use a sterilized seed germinating mix. Moisten it well and fill a flat or pot. Sow seeds at the depth recommended on the packet. Many herbs can also be acquired or shared from cuttings or divisions.

CONTAINER PLANTING AND DESIGN

Planting herbs doesn't require any specialized skill. Most important, moisten the potting mix thoroughly before placing the plants. Use warm to hot water, and stir the soil to make sure all of it is wet. Set transplants at the same depth as they were in their pots. The secret to bounteous, burgeoning containers is to space plants closely, or about 8 inches apart. For the few herbs that do not transplant well, sow directly into the pot, covering lightly with the moistened potting mix; thin the plants after the seeds sprout and develop several sets of leaves.

To create a container planting with a number of different herbs, consider their ultimate height and width, growing habits, and growing requirements. Certain herbs, such as lavender, need a higher pH, and

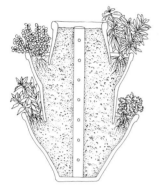

Perhaps you've coveted a terracotta "strawberry jar" planter with lushly growing herbs spilling out of its little side pockets, but you've not had any success growing your own. The trick is to get water distributed throughout the jar. To do this, cut a length of 2-inch PVC pipe the height of your jar. With an electric drill, make ½-inch holes at 4-inch intervals along the length of the pipe. Set the pipe in the middle of the empty strawberry jar and fill with coarse gravel. Holding the pipe, fill in around it with potting soil, inserting plants as each level is filled.

Pinching out the tips of herbs such as basil encourages side branching and prevents the plants from flowering and going to seed.

rosemary has very specific moisture requirements. These are best grown separately. Mints can be rambunctious, even in pots, so it's usually best to grow them in individual pots, as well.

In selecting herbs for a mixed planting, choose one or two that are fairly tall for the center of the container. Herbs of medium height can encircle these. Finally, choose some herbs that creep or sprawl for planting around the edges.

Placement of containers can take full advantage of the smallest of sunny spots, even if the rest of the garden is shady. With casters, a container can be moved around to various areas, where sunlight is abundant or where aesthetics demands. One of the most attractive ways to use containers as a landscape feature is to group pots of various sizes and shapes at different levels.

KEEPING PLANTS HEALTHY AND ATTRACTIVE

The major caveat to the ease of container gardening is making sure plants get enough water, as containers always dry out more quickly than garden soil. Even though most herbs need to have the soil dry out slightly between waterings, in the heat of summer that can mean checking them every day. When the top inch or so of the soil is dry, thoroughly soak the soil, watering from the top. Watering in the morning is best, but do it whenever plants show signs of wilting. Even if you're not a morning person, checking the containers each day, releasing the scents as you brush against them, is a pleasant way to start the day.

As mentioned before, herbs in containers need to be fertilized regularly to keep them producing throughout the growing season. Other maintenance for herbs is minimal. Pinching out the growing tips of the various basils produces side branches and prevents them from flowering and going to seed. For cooking with herbs, harvest leaves any time you want them. For drying or otherwise preserving, the flavor is usually best right before flowering.

Fortunately, herbs are seldom bothered by pests. Dill, fennel, and parsley are hosts to the swallowtail caterpillars. Rather than destroy these future butterflies, grow enough for both you and them. If whiteflies or other insects appear on your herbs, either wash them off with a strong spray of water or use an insecticidal soap spray. Scale can be a problem with bay; the only recourse is to wipe off each little bump on the stems and undersides of leaves with rubbing alcohol or insecticidal soap. Santolina, planted amongst your culinary herbs, is a very effective insect repellent. Rub its leaves everyday to release the powerful scent.

Arranging large pots of herbs on various levels creates a sense of depth and spatial enclosure on an outdoor patio.

To get extra weeks of growth in the fall and spring from an outdoor container planting, protect the plants at night with a cover such as this specially made clear "umbrella."

OVERWINTERING HERBS OUTDOORS

Which herbs can be overwintered outdoors depends on the plant itself as well as your climate. In warmer climates, many herbs, both annual and perennial, can be grown outdoors in containers practically year-round. Where freezing winter temperatures are common, the options are more limited.

Annuals — those plants that grow and die in one growing season — are best enjoyed and used during that period. Pots of annual herbs may also be brought indoors or started from new plantings in the fall for winter use. Perennial herbs — those that grow, die back during the winter, and re-sprout in the spring year after year — may be treated in several different ways. For the least bother, simply let the plants go dormant in the fall, then store the containers in a sheltered spot outdoors or in an unheated garage or cellar. Bring them out in

An inexpensive cold frame can be made from bales of hay (top) or leftover lumber (bottom) and covered with a window sash or a sheet of clear plastic.

A cold frame helps extend the herb growing season.

the spring when new growth starts, feeding and watering regularly. Some perennial herbs, such as thyme or chives, can be brought indoors for use during the winter.

Using a Cold Frame

Another way to extend the growing season is to use a cold frame. Basically, this is a mini-greenhouse about 1 foot to 18 inches tall and 2 by 4 feet or so. Do-it-yourselfers can make their own from lumber or bales of straw and a window sash or a sheet of clear plastic. Local and mail-order garden suppliers offer ready-made alternatives that are relatively inexpensive, easy to set up, and well insulated.

To make the cold frame even more amenable to growing herbs in the winter, you can bury a heating cable in the soil; with this addition, a cold frame becomes known as a hot bed. You can either grow herbs directly in the soil in a cold frame year-round or sink pots of herbs into the soil in a cold frame in the fall. Short, hardy herbs are the best for a cold frame; these include chives, parsley, thyme, rosemary, garlic chives, chervil, and sage. Invest in an automatic opener for the lid, so that the heat doesn't build up inside on warm, sunny winter days. Remember to water the plants, and throw an old rug or heavy blanket over the cold frame on particularly cold nights.

An inexpensive alternative for extending the growing season of potted herbs is a clear, umbrella-like device sold locally or through mail-order sources specifically for this purpose (see page 166 for source).

Growing Herbs Indoors

At the risk of being spoilsports, we are not going to blithely dither on about the effortlessness of growing herbs indoors. The harsh reality is that in general they are not the easiest of plants to keep flourishing inside. But it is not impossible, and the rewards are certainly worth the effort.

Herbs can either be grown indoors year-round, brought inside from the outdoors in the fall, or newly started in the fall. Large planters may be heavy to move, or indoor space may be too small; individual pots are generally the best bet.

The key to successfully growing herbs indoors is bright light. A large window facing south is best, with an eastern exposure the next choice. If you cannot provide the necessary light but want herbs, consider investing in a grow-light unit. This may be a simple fluorescent work light with 4-foot tubes, one warm- and one cool-white. Verilux bulbs provide a better spectrum of light but are much more expensive. Those who are really serious about growing herbs indoors should consider a high-pressure light unit, perhaps also with a matching hydroponic setup as well. To be effective, fluorescent lights should be lit for at least 15 to 16 hours per day.

Next, most herbs need cool temperatures — in the 60° to 70°F range during the day and cooler at night. Maybe everyone should grow herbs indoors so that we think about conserving energy again.

Good air circulation is important to healthy indoor herb growth. That doesn't mean putting them near a heat vent. Instead, invest in a small fan to gently keep the air moving.

Because the herbs won't be as actively growing as in the summer, fertilize less often but continue letting them dry out slightly between regular waterings. Because most of our homes are dry during the winter, increase the humidity around the plants by using a room or whole-house humidifier. Alternatively, set the herbs on either commercially available trays that hold water and have raised racks for holding the pots, or on trays filled with pebbles or capillary matting.

(Above) Many herbs can be grown indoors in a large south-facing window. (Below) Herbs can be grown indoors under grow-lights.

Preserving Herbs

With a sunny room, coldframe, or grow-lamps, plus the availability of herbs at the grocery store, it's possible to have at least some fresh herbs year-round. But the harsh reality is that, except in the mildest of climates, you won't have the same wide range of fresh herbs at your fingertips during the winter months. Even with only a small space

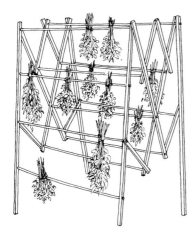

To dry herbs, hang small bunches, upside-down, in a warm, dark, well-ventilated place.

Once the herbs are thoroughly dry, strip the leaves and store them in glass jars.

allotted to growing herbs, there is usually abundance enough for using during the summer, plus enough to harvest and dry for the kitchen in winter.

Drying Herbs

Drying is the easiest and most common way to preserve herbs. For the best flavor, harvest just before the plants bloom, but don't hesitate to harvest at other times if that's more convenient. Pick the herbs in early morning after the dew has dried. Gently wash the herbs, if necessary, and dry in a towel.

Small bunches may be hung up to dry in a warm, dark, well-ventilated place. When thoroughly dry, the leaves are stripped and stored in glass jars. Alternatively, strip the leaves from the stems and place in a dehydrator, or air dry on screens, or between sheets of paper towel, or place on a baking sheet in an oven with a pilot light or set to the lowest possible setting. Store in glass jars as with the hanging method. Drying time for any of these methods varies with the moisture in the plants and humidity levels. When using dried herbs in place of fresh herbs, you may want to reduce the amount by one-third.

Other Preserving Methods

Some herbs lose flavor when dried, especially the basils, tarragon, and chervil. These are better preserved in several other ways. One is to fill a clean glass jar with the herbs and pour in white wine vinegar to cover. Another is to purée the herbs with a small amount of water and freeze in ice cube trays, then store the herb cubes in a freezer container or plastic bag. Fresh herb leaves can also be put directly into freezer bags and kept in the freezer. You can then remove the desired quantity from the freezer as needed.

Anise

Pimpinella anisum

Annual. Feathery, bright green leaves on angular stalks to 2 feet tall with flat clusters of tiny yellow-white edible flowers. Full sun. Standard potting mix; keep evenly moist and fertilize regularly. Start from seeds or transplants. Transplant carefully so as not to disturb roots. Best in large mixed container plantings. Use leaves or flowers anytime available; cut off seed heads when brown, but before they open.

Indoors: Bright light and cool temperatures. Don't expect plants to get very large; use young fresh leaves.

Anise Hyssop, Anise Mint, Mexican Hyssop

Agastache foeniculum

Perennial hardy to -40°F. Erect shrubby plants 2 to 4 feet tall with pointed oval green leaves and spikes of tiny blue-purple edible flowers in late summer and fall. Full sun. Standard potting mix; keep evenly moist and fertilize regularly. Start from transplants or divisions. Grow in 14-inch pots or in mixed container plantings, set near the center. Pinch back plants in early summer to encourage branching. After first bloom, cut plants back by half for a second flowering. Overwinter outdoors in a protected location. Use leaves or flowers anytime available.

Indoors: Not recommended

Arugula, Regula, Roquette, Rucola

Eruca vesicaria subsp. *sativa*

Annual, 6 inches at harvest, can reach 2 feet. Dark green leaves resembling oakleaf lettuce with spikes of tiny white edible flowers. Full sun in early spring and fall, or light shade in summer. Grows best in cool weather. Standard potting mix; keep evenly moist and fertilize regularly. Start from seeds. Grow in pots 10 to 12 inches in diameter or with other salad herbs. Harvest leaves when young, as early as 2 weeks after planting; start new plantings every 2 to 3 weeks to ensure steady supply.

Indoors: Bright light and cool temperatures.

Basil

Ocimum species and cultivars

Annual. Bushy plants ranging in height from 6 inches to 3 feet, with oval pointed leaves ½ to 6 inches long and tiny white or purple edible flowers. Full sun. Standard potting mix; keep evenly moist and fertilize regularly. Start from seeds or transplants. Grow dwarf varieties in 8- to 10-inch pots and larger varieties in pots at least 10 inches in diameter. Use basils in mixed plantings if the container is fairly large and plants get plenty of light and air circulation. To grow six to eight basils together, select a container at least 18 to 20 inches in diameter and 8 to 10 inches deep. Pinch growth to encourage branching, and pick off flower stems to keep the plants producing foliage. Harvest leaves or flowers anytime available.

Indoors: Very bright light and warm temperatures. Dwarf varieties do best.

Bay

Laurus nobilis

Evergreen tree, 3 to 25 feet tall depending on climate, hardy to 20°F. Stiff, dark green pointed oval leaves. Full sun; light shade in hot climates. Standard potting mix; keep evenly moist and fertilize regularly. Start from transplants. Grow young plants in 6-inch pots, repotting into progressively larger pots as needed. Train as a multiple-stemmed shrub or to a single trunk. Bay is very susceptible to scale insects; to remedy, swab all leaf and stem surfaces with rubbing alcohol or insecticidal soap. Harvest leaves anytime.

Indoors: Bright light and cool temperatures.

Bee Balm, Bergamot, Oswego Tea

Monarda didyma

Perennial hardy to -30°F. Bushy, upright plants 2 to 3 feet tall, with 2 to 3-inch oval pointed leaves and unusually shaped edible flowers in shades of pink, magenta, scarlet, purple, or white in midsummer. Full sun to light shade; shade is especially important in hot southern climates. Standard potting mix; keep evenly moist and fertilize

regularly. Start from transplants or divisions. Grow in a 14-inch pot or mixed container planting, set near the center. Keep mildew in check by cutting plants back to 6 inches after blooming; this also encourages a second flowering. Overwinter outdoors in a protected location. Harvest leaves or flowers anytime available.
Indoors: Not recommended.

Borage
Borago officinalis

Annual. Hairy gray-green leaves on floppy stems 18 to 24 inches tall with star-shaped sky-blue edible flowers. Full sun. Standard potting mix; keep evenly moist and fertilize regularly. Start from seeds, directly planted in container because of taproot; self-sows. Matures quickly, so start new plantings once a month during the summer. Grow in a 12-inch pot or as mixed container plants, set in the background. Use leaves when young or flowers when available.
Indoors: Not recommended.

Burnet, Salad Burnet
Poterium sanguisorba

Perennial hardy to -35°F; evergreen in areas with mild winters or when protected by a cold frame. Fernlike leaves in mounds 10 inches tall, with stems of 1-inch rounded clusters of tiny pink edible flowers rising above. Full sun to light shade. Standard potting mix; keep evenly moist and fertilize regularly. Start from seeds or

transplants. Grow in pots 10 to 12 inches in diameter or in a large mixed container, planted toward the center. Overwinter in a protected location. Use leaves or flowers anytime available. A cold frame is the best method for winter production.
Indoors: Bright light and cool temperatures.

Caraway
Carum carvi

Biennial. Feathery leaves on floppy stems to 2 feet long with flat clusters of tiny white edible flowers. Full sun. Standard potting mix; keep evenly moist and fertilize regularly. Start from seeds, sown directly in container; self-sows. Does best in cool weather. In climates with a winter minimum of 20°F, sow seeds in the fall. Use a 12- to 14-inch pot at least 10 inches deep for 6 to 7 plants or add several plants to a mixed container planting, setting plants near the edge. Use leaves or flowers anytime available; cut off seed heads when brown, but before they open; harvest roots after gathering seeds. A cold frame is the best method for winter production.
Indoors: Bright light and very cool temperatures will provide fresh foliage.

Chervil
Anthriscus cerefolium

Annual. Grows 12 inches tall, with finely textured fernlike leaves and clusters of tiny white edible flowers. Light shade.

Standard potting mix; keep evenly moist and fertilize regularly. Start from seeds, sown directly in container. Grow several plants in a 12-inch pot, or place toward the center of mixed plantings. Will burn in hot summer sun. Does best in cool weather. Make successive plantings in spring and fall, with harvest of the outside leaves starting 6 weeks after planting. Pinch out emerging flower stalks to prolong foliage growth. Excellent for growing in a cold frame, as it is hardy to 30°F.
Indoors: Bright light and cool temperatures. Make successive plantings.

Chile Pepper
Capsicum species

Tender perennial. Shrubby plants growing 1 to 3 feet tall with green fruit ½ to 6 inches long ripening to red, yellow, or purple, depending on the variety. Full sun. Standard potting mix; keep evenly moist and fertilize frequently. Start from seeds or transplants. Grow taller varieties in pots at least 12 inches in diameter; smaller-growing ornamental peppers, which have very hot edible fruit, combine well in mixed plantings. Harvest fruit at any stage.
Indoors: Not recommended.

Chives
Allium schoenoprasum

Perennial hardy to -40°F. Clumps of slender hollow leaves 12 to 18 inches tall with 1-inch spherical mauve-colored edible flowers in early summer. Full sun. Standard potting mix; keep evenly moist and fertilize regularly. Start from seeds, transplants, or divisions. Grow in 12-inch pots or mixed container plantings, placed toward the outer edge. A cold frame is the best method for winter production. Harvest leaves or flowers anytime available.

Indoors: Bright light and cool temperatures. Start seeds in the fall for winter use; the variety 'Grolau' is especially recommended for indoor growing. Before using a pot of chives brought in from outdoors, a dormant period is necessary. Leave them outdoors until Christmas; then cut back, bring indoors, feed, and water.

Clove Pinks, Pinks, Carnation, Gillflower

Dianthus caryophyllus
Perennial hardy to 10°F.; may be grown as an annual. Thin, gray-blue leaves form 12-inch mounds with 18-inch stems of edible red, pink, or white flowers in spring. Full sun. Standard potting mix; keep evenly moist and fertilize regularly. Start from transplants for bloom the first year. Growth is best in the cool weather of spring and fall. Remove faded flowers to encourage additional blooming. Grow in 12-inch pots or in mixed plantings, placing them toward the edge to the middle of the planter. Use flowers when available.

Indoors: Not recommended unless with very bright light and very cool temperatures.

Coriander, Cilantro

Coriandrum sativum
Hardy annual. Flat, parsley-like leaves on floppy stems to 24 inches with open clusters of tiny pink-white edible flowers. Full sun. Standard potting mix; keep soil evenly moist and fertilize regularly. Start from seeds, sown directly into a 12-inch pot; make successive plantings every month as plants mature quickly; self-sows. Grows well in a cold frame during the winter. Use leaves or flowers anytime available; cut off seed heads when brown, but before they open.

Indoors: Bright light and cool temperatures. Start seeds in the fall for wintering indoors, making successive plantings. Will not mature to flowers in winter months.

Cress

Lepidum sativum
(Garden cress)
Nasturtium officinalis
(Watercress)
Garden cress is a fast-growing annual, with small bright-green leaves. Full sun in spring and fall; light shade during hotter months. Standard potting mix; keep evenly moist and fertilize regularly. Start from seeds. Make successive plantings of seeds sprinkled in 12-inch pots, or combine seeds with those of arugula, mache, and other salad herbs for a mixed planter. Harvest leaves when 4 to 6 inches tall; flavor is best in cool weather.

Watercress is a biennial hardy to -20°F. Bright green, oval, toothed leaves on stems to 12 inches tall and clusters of small white edible flowers. Full sun to light shade. Start from transplants. Grow in 6- to 10-inch pots set out in early spring. Water daily or set in tubs of water that are changed daily. Flavor of leaves is best in cool weather.

Indoors: Make successive plantings of garden cress in pots, providing bright light and cool temperatures. Growing watercress indoors is not recommended.

Daylily

Hemerocallis species and cultivars
Perennial hardy to -40°F. Clumps of grass-like leaves 18 inches to 6 feet tall and leafless stalks with clusters of edible lily-like flowers in shades of yellow, apricot, or burgundy. Full sun or semi-shade. Standard potting mix; keep evenly moist and fertilize regularly. Start from transplants or divisions. Grow in pots at least 12 inches in diameter or in large mixed plantings, set toward the center. Overwinter outdoors in a protected location. Use flowers when available.

Indoors: Not recommended.

Dill

Anethum graveolens
Annual. Blue-green, fine-textured foliage on angular, hollow stems 18 to 48 inches tall with flat clusters of tiny yellow edible flowers. Full sun, or light shade in hot climates. Standard potting mix; keep

evenly moist and fertilize regularly. Start from seeds, sown directly in containers; self-sows. Grow in 12-inch or larger pots or in mixed container plantings, set toward the center. Make successive plantings from early spring to early summer and again in late summer to fall. In warm climates, sow seed in the fall for early spring growth. Use leaves or flowers anytime available; harvest seed heads when brown, but before they open.
Indoors: Bright light and cool temperatures. Make successive plantings.

Fennel
Foeniculum vulgare
Perennial hardy to -15°F.; often grown as an annual. Fine-textured, light-green or bronze leaves on angular, branching pithy stems growing

3 to 5 feet tall with flat-topped clusters of tiny yellow edible flowers. Full sun. Standard potting mix; keep evenly moist and fertilize regularly. Start from seeds; self-sows. Grow several in a 14-inch pot, spacing 4 to 6 inches apart, or in a mixed planter, set toward the center. In warmer climates, sow seed in the fall for early spring growth. Overwinter outdoors in a protected location. Use leaves or flowers anytime available; harvest seed heads when brown, but before they open.
Indoors: Bright light and moderate to cool temperatures. Start new plants in the fall for indoor growing.

Garlic
Allium sativum
Bulb hardy to -40°F. Flat, sword-like, gray-green leaves 18 to 24 inches long with a single-stemmed sphere of small white flowers.

Full sun. Standard potting mix; keep evenly moist and fertilize regularly. Plant individual cloves, pointed end up, 1 inch deep in the fall while temperatures are still warm, spacing 4 inches apart in a 12- to 16-inch container. The following summer, remove the flower stem and harvest the bulb when the first six leaves turn brown. After pulling up the bulbs, shake off the loose soil and cut off the stringy roots. Place on screens or hang the entire plant to dry in a warm, dark, well-ventilated place. After several weeks, remove the top. Alternatively, let the bulbs dry for a day or two, soak the tops in water for an hour, then braid 18 or so bulbs together and hang to dry. Use garlic cloves anytime or the whole plant when young.
Indoors: Not recommended.

Garlic Chives
Allium tuberosum
Perennial hardy to -40°F; evergreen in warmer climates. Clumps of thin, flat, grass-like leaves 18 inches tall and clusters of small

white edible flowers on single stems. Full sun. Standard potting mix; keep evenly moist and fertilize regularly. Start from seeds, transplants, or divisions. Grow in 12-inch pots or in mixed container plantings, set toward

the edge. Overwinter in a protected location. Excellent for growing in a cold frame. Use leaves or flowers anytime available.
Indoors: Bright light and cool temperatures. Start new plantings in the fall from divisions.

Ginger
Zingiber officinale
Perennial hardy to 25°F. Stiff, angular stems 2 to 4 feet tall with long, thin, pointed leaves. Light shade. Standard potting

mix; keep evenly moist and fertilize regularly. Start plants with roots purchased from a supermarket produce department, selecting large, plump ones with well-developed "eyes." Lay the root on its side in a 10- to 12-inch pot; cover with ½ to 1 inch of soil; keep warm and moist until sprouted. In late fall, bring indoors and grow as a houseplant. Or, cut plants back to the ground and let them rest in a cool, dark place; bring into warmth and light and begin watering and feeding in late winter or early spring. Harvest roots 8 to 12 months after planting, either cutting off a section or harvesting the entire crop.
Indoors: Bright light, warm temperatures, and high humidity.

Horseradish
Armoracia rusticana
Perennial hardy to -20°F. Strap-like leaves 1 to 2 feet long with 2- to 3-foot spikes of tiny white edible flowers. Full sun. Standard

potting mix; keep evenly moist and fertilize regularly. Start from transplants or divisions. Grow alone in a 14- to 16-inch container. Overwinter outdoors in a protected location. Use young leaves or flowers when available. Harvest roots in late fall when 1 to 2 years old.
Indoors: Not recommended.

Hyssop

Hyssopus officinalis
Semi-evergreen to evergreen woody perennial hardy to -30°F. Branching shrub 18 to 24 inches tall with narrow, dark green, 1-inch-

long leaves and 6-inch spikes of tiny blue, white, or pink edible flowers. Full sun. Standard potting mix; allow to dry out slightly between thorough waterings; fertilize regularly. Start from transplants. Grow in 12-inch pots or in large mixed containers, set toward the center. Overwinter outdoors in a protected location. Use leaves or flowers anytime available.
Indoors: Bright light and cool temperatures.

Lavender

Lavandula species and cultivars
Annual or perennial, depending on variety and growing conditions; English lavender (*L. angustifolia*) is hardy

to -10°F but subject to winterkill if the soil is not well- drained; growth is poor in hot, humid summers. Bushy, branching plants with fine-textured, gray-green leaves and spikes of tiny purple, lavender, white, or pink edible

flowers. Depending on the variety, plants grow 1 to 3 feet tall. Full sun. Standard potting mix with a pH of 7 to 8. Let the soil dry out slightly between thorough waterings. Fertilize regularly. Start from transplants. Grow in 10- to 12-inch pots or in mixed containers if other herbs can tolerate the same pH. Where hardy, English lavender can sometimes be overwintered in pots outdoors if a handful of lime is added to the soil in the fall after blooming; trim plants in early spring or after flowering in early summer. Use flowers when available; regular harvesting encourages additional flowering.
Indoors: Bright light and cool temperatures; French lavender *L. dentata)* is best for growing indoors.

Lemon Balm

Melissa officinalis
Perennial hardy to -20°F. Mounded plant growing 18 to 24 inches tall with 2- to 3-inch rough-textured, oval, scalloped leaves with

small white edible flowers. Full sun to light shade. Standard potting mix; keep evenly moist and fertilize regularly. Start from seeds, transplants, divisions, or stem cuttings. Grow in 12- to 14-inch pots. Remove blooms to keep plants from going to seed and self-sowing. Overwinter outdoors in a protected location. Use leaves or flowers anytime available.
Indoors: Bright light and cool temperatures.

Lemongrass

Cymbopogon citratus
Annual. Clumps of grass-like leaves 2 to 3 feet tall. Full sun. Standard potting mix. Drought-tolerant but best if soil is kept evenly moist and well-drained. Grow in a 14-inch pot or in a large mixed container, set toward the center. Start from transplants or divisions; or, root stems bought at the grocery by re-cutting the base, putting in a glass of water, and potting up when roots form in about 2 weeks. In colder climates grow as an annual, overwinter indoors, or store dormant in a frost-free place with occasional watering. Harvest by removing the stem at the base, cutting or peeling off leaves (which can be brewed for tea), and using the tender inner stalk.
Indoors: Bright light and moderate temperatures.

Lemon Verbena

Aloysia triphylla
Deciduous woody shrub hardy to 25°F. Sprawling plant, 5 to 15 feet tall, with narrow light-green leaves 2 to 4 inches long in whorls

around the stem and tiny heliotrope-scented edible flowers in late summer. Full sun. Standard potting mix; keep soil moist and fertilize regularly. Start from transplants or cuttings. Grow in a pot at least 12 inches in diameter. Wash leaves weekly to prevent spider mites and whiteflies; if infested, treat with insecticidal soap spray. After leaves drop in autumn, bring it indoors after the first frost, prune off about

one-third of the growth, and keep in a dimly lit spot at 55°F, watering occasionally. In late winter, bring into bright light and keep soil evenly moist. Use leaves or flowers when available.

Lovage
Levisticum officinale

Perennial hardy to -40°F. Hollow stems growing 6 feet tall with celery-like leaves and flat clusters of tiny yellow edible flowers in midsummer. Full sun to light shade. Standard potting mix; keep soil evenly moist and fertilize regularly. Start from seeds, transplants, or divisions. Grow in a pot at least 14 inches in diameter or at the center of a large mixed container planting. If plants become infested with aphids, treat with insecticidal soap spray. Overwintered outdoors in a protected location, lovage is one of the first plants to sprout in the spring. Use leaves or flowers anytime available.
Indoors: Not recommended.

Marjoram
Origanum majorana, O. majoricum

Perennial; *O. majorana* is hardy to 20°F . It may be grown as an annual. Velvety oval leaves ¼ to 1 inch long on sprawling to erect plants 12 to 18 inches tall with rounded clusters of pink or mauve edible flowers in late summer. Full sun, or light shade in hotter climates. Standard potting mix with a pH of 7 to 8. Allow soil to dry out slightly

between thorough waterings. Fertilize regularly. Start from transplants, woody cuttings, or divisions. Grow in 10-inch pots or in mixed container plantings, set near the edge. Use leaves or flowers anytime available.
Indoors: Excellent houseplant for bright light and mild to cool temperatures.

Mexican Marigold
Tagetes lucida

Perennial hardy to 0°F; may be grown as an annual. Bushy plant 30 to 36 inches tall with narrow pointed leaves 2 to 3 inches long, with clusters of golden 1-inch edible flowers in fall. Full sun. Standard potting mix; keep evenly moist and fertilize regularly. Start from seeds or transplants; self-sows; cuttings root in water. Grow in 10-inch pots or in the center of a mixed container planting. Use leaves or flowers anytime available.
Indoors: Excellent houseplant for bright light and moderate temperatures.

Mint
Mentha species and cultivars

Perennials hardy to -25°F. Bushy plants growing 18 to 36 inches tall with pointed, toothed leaves 1 to 2 inches long. The exceptions are Corsican mint and pennyroyal, both of which are hardy to 10°F, grow close to the ground, and have tiny round leaves. All mints have square stems and spikes of tiny purple, pink, or white edible

flowers in midsummer. Full sun to light shade. Standard potting mix; keep evenly moist and fertilize regularly. Seed-started mints vary greatly, so it is best to buy transplants or take cuttings or divisions. Grow in pots at least 12 inches in diameter. Overwinter in a protected location outdoors.
Indoors: Bright light and cool temperatures for peppermint. Spearmint does not grow well indoors.

Nasturtium
Tropaeolum majus

Annual, hardy to 30°F. Bushy plants 8 to 18 inches tall or vines 6 feet long or more, with 2-inch round, green or variegated leaves and 2-inch red, orange, mahogany, yellow, or cream-colored edible flowers. Full sun, or light shade in hotter climates. Standard potting mix. Let soil dry out slightly between thorough waterings. Start from seeds; plant directly into pots, soaking seeds in water overnight before planting. Depending on variety, grow in a 12-inch pot on hanging basket, or at the edge of a mixed container planting. Or, train vining varieties on a trellis. Trim back plants if they get leggy. Control aphids by washing off with a hard spray of water or insecticidal soap spray. Use leaves or flowers anytime available.
Indoors: Bright light and cool to moderate temperatures. Start seeds in late summer or fall for growing indoors in winter.

Oregano

Origanum vulgare var. *prismaticum*

Perennial hardy to -20°F. Bushy plants 1 to 2 feet tall, with small rounded leaves and branching clusters of tiny white edible flowers in late summer. Full sun. Standard potting mix; keep evenly moist and fertilize regularly. Start from transplants or cuttings. Grow in a 10- to 12-inch pot or in mixed container plantings. Use leaves or flowers anytime available.
Indoors: Bright light and cool temperatures.

Parsley

Petroselinum crispum

Biennial hardy to -10°F. Rounded plants growing 8 to 12 inches tall, with flat or curly leaves. Full sun to light shade. Standard potting mix; keep evenly moist and fertilize regularly. Start from seeds or transplants. Seeds are slow to germinate, sometimes taking 3 weeks; to speed germination, soak the seeds in water overnight. Transplant when young because of the taproot. Grow in 10- to 14-inch pots or mixed container plantings. The caterpillars of swallowtail butterflies eat parsley as well as dill and fennel; grow enough for both you and them. Plants remain green when overwintered in a cold frame or mulched with leaves or straw, but they quickly flower and die the following spring.
Indoors: Bright light and cool temperatures. Either bring in a pot from outdoors or start new plants from seed in late summer or fall.

Pot Marigold

Calendula officinalis

Annual hardy to 25°F.; can be planted outdoors in the fall in mild climates. Branching plants grow 8 to 24 inches tall, with smooth oblong leaves and single or double daisy-like edible flowers 2 to 3 inches across in shades of yellow, gold, orange, and apricot. Full sun, or light shade in hot climates. Standard potting mix; keep evenly moist and fertilize regularly. Start from seeds or transplants; self-sows. Control whiteflies and aphids by washing off with a strong spray of water or insecticidal soap spray. Harvest flowers regularly for use and repeat bloom.
Indoors: Bright light and cool temperatures. Bring pots in from outdoors or start new plants from seed in mid-to-late summer.

Rosemary

Rosmarinus officinalis

Perennial hardy to -10° or -20°F, depending on variety. Woody shrub growing to 3 feet or more tall, with stiff narrow 1-inch leaves and edible blue flowers; trailing or creeping and pink- or white-flowered varieties are also available. Full sun. Standard potting mix, with a pH of 7 to 8; keep evenly moist and fertilize regularly. Start from transplants or cuttings. Grow in a 12-inch or larger pot or in a mixed container planting. 'Arp' and 'Hardy Hill' are considered the hardiest varieties. In colder climates, bring plants indoors.
Indoors: Bright light and cool temperatures; soil must be well drained but never allowed to dry out.

Sage

Salvia officinalis

Woody shrub hardy to -20°F; fruit varieties are treated as annuals. Bushy plants 12 to 30 inches tall. Rough-textured grey-green, deep green, purple, or variegated leaves with tiny lavender edible flowers. Full sun. Standard potting mix; keep evenly moist and fertilize regularly; tolerates some drought. Start from transplants or cuttings. Grow in a 12-inch pot or in a mixed container. Replace sage every three or four years, as plants become woody with less foliage. Grows well in a cold frame in winter. Alternatively, overwinter outdoors in a protected location. Harvest leaves or flowers anytime available.
Indoors: Bright light and cool temperatures. Keep soil slightly dry without letting it dry completely.

Santolina

Santolina chamaecyparissus (Gray); *Santolina viridis* (Green)

Not a culinary herb, but recommended as the best natural bug repellent. Can be grown individually in buckets around the patio, or planted on the edge of larger containers. Needs full sun. Start from transplants. It grows very vigorously without much moisture or fertilization. Rub or brush it, which will release the essential oils and the fragrance that keeps the insects away from your patio or porch. Also keeps insects away when you're barbecuing. Trim slightly in late summer. Several species of the gray, 'Pretty Carrol' and *Neopolitanum* are a little more feathery than the standard santolina. **Indoors:** Bright sun in day and very cool at night.

Savory, Summer

Satureja hortensis
Annual. Sprawling plants 18 to 24 inches tall with tender gray-green 1-inch leaves and tiny pinkish-white edible flowers in midsummer. Full sun. Standard potting mix; keep evenly moist and fertilize regularly. Start from seeds or transplants. Grow in 12-inch pots or mixed planters, set near the edge. To keep growth upright, use plant support rings. Pinch out flowers to keep foliage growing. Use leaves or flowers anytime available. **Indoors:** Bright light and cool temperatures.

Savory, Winter

Satureja montana
Semi-evergreen perennial hardy to -10°F. Bushy plants 6 to 12 inches tall with glossy, dark green leaves. Full sun. Standard potting mix; keep soil evenly moist and fertilize regularly. Start from transplants. Grow in 10-inch pots or mixed containers, planted near the edge. A trailing variety is good in hanging baskets and at the edge of mixed containers. Overwinter in a cold frame or a protected location. Use leaves anytime available. **Indoors:** Bright light and cool temperatures.

Scented Geraniums

Pelargonium species and cultivars
Annual. Rangy plants 18 to 36 inches tall; depending on variety, leaves vary in size, shape, texture, and scent, with rose, mint, and fruit the most popular; occasional pink or white edible flowers. Full sun to light shade. Standard potting mix; keep evenly moist and fertilize regularly, but do not overfeed. Start from transplants or cuttings taken in spring or fall. Plant in 10- to 16-inch pots. Use leaves or flowers anytime available.
Indoors: Bright light and moderate temperatures. Good air circulation is important. When bringing indoors in the fall, cut larger variety plants back to 12 inches.

Shallot, Eschallot

Allium cepa
Perennial hardy to -40°F. Hollow, onion-like leaves to 12 inches tall. Full sun. Standard potting mix; keep evenly moist and fertilize regularly. Grow in containers at least 12 to 16 inches across and deep. Plant bulbs in late summer, with the pointed end up and one-third above the soil. Overwinter in a protected location outdoors. Harvest bulbs the following summer when leaves begin to yellow and die. Dry bulbs and store in mesh bags. Use leaves anytime plant has achieved good size.
Indoors: Not recommended.

Signet Marigold

Tagetes signata
(T. tenuifolia)
Annual. Spreading 10-inch mounds of small delicate leaves and ½- to 1-inch yellow, orange, or gold edible flowers. Full sun. Standard potting mix; keep soil evenly moist and fertilize regularly. Start from seeds or transplants. Grow in containers 12 inches across or in mixed planters near the edge. Keep blooms picked for continued flowering. Use flowers when available.
Indoors: Bright light and cool temperatures.

Sorrel

Rumex species
Perennial hardy to
-40°F. Garden,
English, or broadleaf
sorrel *(R. acetosa)* has
8- to 12-inch broad,
lance-shaped leaves;
French sorrel

(R. scutalus) has 2-inch lance-shaped
leaves. Full sun, or part shade in hot
climates. Standard potting mix; keep
evenly moist and fertilize regularly.
Start from seeds, sown directly into
containers, or transplants. Grow in a
pot 12 inches in diameter. Overwinter
in a protected location. French sorrel
has the better flavor and can be grown
in a cold frame. Harvest young leaves
throughout the growing season,
cutting leaves at the base of the plant.
Indoors: Not recommended.

Sweet Cicely

Myrrhis odorata
Perennial hardy to
-30°F. Branching
plant 18 to 30 inches
in height with
fernlike leaves and
2-inch clusters of
tiny white edible
flowers. Shade or

light shade in cool climates. Standard
potting mix; keep evenly moist and
fertilize regularly. Start from
transplants. Grow in 12- to 16-inch
pots or in mixed planters with other
shade-loving herbs. Use leaves
throughout the growing season;
harvest seed heads when brown, but
before they open; harvest roots in the
fall. Overwinter containers in a
protected location.
Indoors: Not recommended.

Tarragon

Artemisia dracunculus
Perennial hardy to
-20°F. Trailing
2-foot stems with
narrow leaves 1 to
2 inches long. Full
sun. Standard
potting mix; keep

evenly moist and fertilize only once
during the growing season, as too
much fertilizer will diminish flavor.
Buy transplants of French tarragon,
which does not produce seed; Russian
tarragon has little flavor. Grow in a
12-inch or larger container.
Overwinter in a protected location.
Use leaves anytime.
Indoors: Not generally
recommended, but a container plant
can be brought indoors after a
minimum 6-week cold period
outdoors (usually by February) and
kept in a cool, bright place. Mexican
marigold is a good indoor substitute.

Thyme

Thymus species and
cultivars
Perennials hardy to
-20°F. Ground-
hugging to rounded
growth from ½ to
15 inches tall with
⅛- to ½-inch oval

green or variegated leaves and tiny
white, pink, or purple edible flowers in
midsummer. Full sun. Standard
potting mix; let the soil dry out
slightly between watering; avoid

getting the foliage wet. Fertilize
regularly. Start from transplants,
cuttings, or divisions. Plant upright
thymes in 10-inch pots. Use creeping
thymes in hanging baskets or mixed
containers, set at the edge. Thymes
grow well in cold frames. If bringing
plants indoors in the fall, trim back
first. Use leaves or flowers anytime
available.
Indoors: Bright light and cool
temperatures. Make sure containers
are well drained.

Violet

Viola odorata
Perennial hardy to
-20°F. Rounded
clumps to 6 inches
tall with heart-
shaped, dark green
leaves and ½- to
1-inch edible flowers

in shades of blue, lavender, pink,
purple, rose, and white. Start from
transplants or divisions. Light
to full shade. Standard potting mix;
keep evenly moist and fertilize
regularly. Grow in 6- to 10-inch pots
or in mixed planters with other shade-
loving herbs. Use flowers or leaves
anytime available. Also consider
growing the related edible-flowered
pansies and Johnny-jump-ups.
Indoors: Bright light and cool
temperatures.

Appendix/Index

Herbs

The following businesses sell herb plants or seeds. Visit one near you, or write for catalogs. Many can ship herb plants to you.

Akin' Back Farm
2501 Highway 53 South
LaGrange, KY 40031

Blue Springs
236 Eleanor Avenue
Los Altos, CA 94022

Brown's Edgeward Gardens
2661 Corrine Drive
Orlando, FL 32803

Cactus Patch Herbs
Route 2, Box 33
Seymour, IN 47274

Caprilands
534 Silver Street
Coventry, CT 06238

Carroll Gardens
P.O. Box 310
Westminster, MD 21157

Chili Pepper Emporium
328 San Felipe N.W.
Albuquerque, NM 87104
(Pepper seeds)

Circle Herb Farm
Route 1, Box 247
East Jordan, MI 49727

Clark's Greenhouse
Route 1, Box 15B
San Jose, IL 62682

Companion Plants
7247 North Coolville Ridge Road
Athens, OH 45701

The Cook's Garden
Box 535
Londonderry, VT 05148
(Herb, edible flower, and gourmet
vegetable seed)

Country Heritage Nurseries
P.O. Box 536
Hartford, MI 49057

Dabney Herbs
Box 22061
Louisville, KY 40252-0061

Filaree Farm
Route 1, Box 162
Okanogan, WA 98840
(Over 50 different garlics)

Forestfarm
990 Tetherow Road
Williams, OR 97544-9599

Fragrant Fields
128 Front Street
Dongola, IL 62926

The Gathered Herb
12114 North State Road
Otisville, MI 48463

Gilbertie's Herb Gardens
Sylvan Lane
Westport, CT 06880

Glade Valley Nursery
9226 Links Road
Walkersville, MD 21793

Goodwin Creek Gardens
P.O. Box 83
Williams, OR 97544

Hartman's Herb Farm
Old Dana Road
Barre, MA 01005

Havasu Hills Herbs
20150 Rough & Ready Trail
Sonora, CA 95370

The Herb Garden
P.O. Box 773
Pilot Mountain, NC 27041-0773

The Herbary & Stuff
Route 3, Box 83
Jacksonville, TX 75766

The Herbfarm
32804 Issaquah-Fall City Road
Fall City, WA 98024

Herbs-Liscious
1702 South Sixth Street
Marshalltown, IA 50158

Hilltop Herb Farm
P.O. Box 325
Romayor, TX 77368
(Do not ship)

The Hollow, Orchids & Herbs
71 German Crossroad
Ithaca, NY 14850
(Do not ship)

Horticultural Enterprises
P.O. Box 810082
Dallas, TX 75381-0082
(Pepper seeds)

Hundley Ridge Farm
Box 253, Squiresville Road
Perry Park, KY 40363
(Do not ship)

It's About Thyme
P.O. Box 878
Manchaca, TX 78652

A Kiss of the Sun Nursery
5273 South Coast Highway
South Beach, OR 97366

Le Jardin du Gourmet
P.O. Box 275
St. Johnsbury Center, VT 05863
(Shallot and garlic sets)

Legacy Herbs
HC 70, Box 442
Mountain View, AR 72560
(Do not ship)

Lewis Mountain Herbs & Everlastings
2345 Street, Route 247
Manchester, OH 45144

Lily of the Valley Herb Farm
3969 Fox Avenue
Minerva, OH 44657

Logee's Greenhouses
141 North Street
Danielson, CT 06239

McClure & Zimmerman
P.O. Box 368
Friesland, WI 53935-0368
(Saffron crocus, garlic, and shallots)

Merry Gardens
P.O. Box 595
Camden, ME 04843-0595

The Natural Gardening Company
217 San Anselmo Avenue
San Anselmo, CA 94960

Niche Gardens
1111 Dawson Road
Chapel Hill, NC 27516

Nichols Garden Nursery
1190 North Pacific Highway
Albany, OR 97321-4598

The Pepper Gal
P.O. Box 12534
Lake Park, FL 33403-0534
(Pepper seeds)

Pinetree Garden Seeds
Box 300
New Gloucester, ME 04260

Plants of the Southwest
Agua Fria, Route 6, Box 11
Santa Fe, NM 87501

Rabbit Shadow Farm
2880 East Highway 402
Loveland, CO 80537
(Herb topiaries)

Rasland Farm
NC 82 at US 13
Godwin, NC 28344-9712

Rose Hill Herbs and Perennials
Route 4, Box 377
Amherst, VA 24521

The Rosemary House
120 South Market Street
Mechanicsburg, PA 17055

Sandy Mush Herb Nursery
Route 2, Surrett Cove Road
Leicester, NC 28748

Shady Hill Gardens
821 Walnut Street
Batavia, IL 60510
(Scented geraniums)

Shepherd's Garden Seeds
6116 Highway 9
Felton, CA 95018
(Herb, edible flower, and gourmet
vegetable seed)

Story House Herb Farm
Route 7, Box 246
Murray, KY 42071

Sunnybrook Farms Nursery
9448 Mayfield Road
Chesterland, OH 44026

Tinmouth Channel Farm
Box 428B, Town Highway 19
Tinmouth, VT 05773

Triple Oaks Nursery
Box 384, Delsea Drive
Franklinville, NJ 08322

Vileniki — An Herb Farm
Route 1, Box 345
Oliphant, PA 18447
(Do not ship)

Well-Sweep Herb Farm
317 Mt. Bethel Road
Port Murray, NJ 07865

Wrenwood of Berkeley Springs
Route 4, Box 361
Berkeley Springs, WV 25411-9413

Organic Gardening Supplies

Age-Old Gardening Supply
P.O. Box 1556
Boulder, CO 80306

Bargyla Rateaver
9049 Covina Street
San Diego, CA 92126

Bountiful Gardens
5798 Ridgewood Road
Willits, CA 95490

Bricker's Organic Farm
842 Sandbar Ferry Road
Augusta, GA 30901

Earlee, Inc.
2002 Highway 62
Jeffersonville, IN 47130-3556

Earthly Goods Farm & Garden Supply
Route 3, Box 761
Mounds, OK 74047

Full Circle Garden Products
P.O. Box 6
Redway, CA 95560

Gardener's Supply Company
128 Intervale Road
Burlington, VT 05401

Gardens Alive!
5100 Schenley Place
Lawrenceburg, IN 47025

Green Earth Organics
9422 144th Street East
Puyallap, WA 98373

Growing Naturally
P.O. Box 54149 Pine Lane
Pineville, PA 18946

Harmony Farm Supply
P.O. Box 460
Grafton, CA 95444

Holland's Organic Garden
8515 Stearns
Overland Park, KS 66214

The Natural Gardening Company
217 San Anselmo Avenue
San Anselmo, CA 94960

Nitron Industries
P.O. Box 1447
Fayetteville, AR 72702

Ohio Earth Food
13737 Duquette Avenue N.E.
Hartville, OH 44632

Organic Control, Inc.
P.O. Box 781147
Los Angeles, CA 90016

Organic Pest Management
P.O. Box 55267
Seattle, WA 98155

Peaceful Valley Farm Supply
P.O. Box 2209
Grass Valley, CA 95945

High Intensity Light and Hydroponic Equipment

HydroFarm Gardening Products
3135 Kerner Boulevard
San Rafael, CA 94901

Cold Frames

Kinsman Company
River Road
Point Pleasant, PA 18950

Simpson Strong-Tie Company
23305 East Highway 3
Rose Lake, ID 83810

Umbrella Cold Frame

Solar Garden Company
Box 909
Cherry Hill Cottage
Stockbridge, MA 01262

Publications

The Herb Companion
Interweave Press
201 East Fourth Street
Loveland, CO 80537
(Bimonthly magazine on growing and using herbs)

The Herb Quarterly
P.O. Box 689
San Anselmo, CA 94960
(Quarterly)

Herban Lifestyles
84 Carpenter Road
New Hartford, CT 06057
(Quarterly)

Converting Recipe Measurements to Metric

Use the following chart for converting U.S. measurements to metric. Since the conversions are not exact, it's important to convert the measurements for all of the ingredients to maintain the same proportions as the original recipe.

To Convert To	When the Measurement Given Is	Multiply It By
milliliters	teaspoons	4.93
milliliters	tablespoons	14.79
milliliters	fluid ounces	29.57
milliliters	cups	236.59
liters	cups	0.236
milliliters	pints	473.18
liters	pints	0.473
milliliters	quarts	946.36
liters	quarts	0.946
liters	gallons	3.785
grams	ounces	28.35
kilograms	pounds	0.454
centimeters	inches	2.54
degrees Celsius	degrees Fahrenheit	$\frac{5}{9}$ (°F − 32)